The World of the Harvester Ants

Number Twenty-Three:
W. L. Moody, Jr., Natural History Series

The World
of the Harvester Ants

by Stephen Welton Taber

TEXAS A&M UNIVERSITY PRESS

COLLEGE STATION

Library of Congress Cataloging-in-Publication Data

Taber, Stephen Welton, 1956–
     The world of the harvester ants / by Stephen Welton
Taber. — 1st ed.
            p.   cm. — (W.L. Moody, Jr., natural history
series ; no. 23)
     Includes bibliographical references and index.
     ISBN 0-89096-815-2
     1. Harvester ants. I. Title. II. Series.
QL568.F7T235   1998
595.79'6—dc21   97-39206
                                                                        CIP

To Elaine

Something in the insect seems to be alien
to the habits, morals,
and psychology of this world,
as if it had come from some other planet, more monstrous,
more energetic, more insensate,
more atrocious, more infernal than our own.

—MAURICE MAETERLINCK

Contents

Illustrations

Species Drawings and Distribution Maps

following page 92

Pogonomyrmex carbonarius
Pogonomyrmex catanlilensis
Pogonomyrmex coarctatus
Pogonomyrmex colei
Pogonomyrmex comanche
Pogonomyrmex desertorum
Pogonomyrmex guatemaltecus
Pogonomyrmex huachucanus
Pogonomyrmex inermis
Pogonomyrmex laticeps
Pogonomyrmex lobatus
Pogonomyrmex longibarbis
Pogonomyrmex magnacanthus
Pogonomyrmex marcusi
Pogonomyrmex maricopa
Pogonomyrmex meridionalis
Pogonomyrmex micans
Pogonomyrmex montanus
Pogonomyrmex occidentalis
Pogonomyrmex pronotalis
Pogonomyrmex rastratus
Pogonomyrmex rugosus
Pogonomyrmex salinus
Pogonomyrmex snellingi
Pogonomyrmex subdentatus
Pogonomyrmex subnitidus
Pogonomyrmex tenuispina
Pogonomyrmex texanus
Pogonomyrmex theresiae
Pogonomyrmex uruguayensis
Pogonomyrmex vermiculatus
Pogonomyrmex wheeleri
Pogonomyrmex species B

Hylomyrma reitteri

Preface

This book is the result of a comprehensive study of the harvester ant genera *Pogonomyrmex* and *Ephebomyrmex*. It began as a large technical monograph, which found no home because of its size and because it contained words that were unfamiliar to most readers. That often happens when one tries to assimilate two hundred years of literature in seven languages from more than twelve hundred books, journals, theses, dissertations, agricultural bulletins, and unpublished manuscripts. The original version was just too large and dry. So it lost some weight and became readable by those who have never heard of a myrmecologist. One such ant biologist was the eccentric nineteenth-century physician-naturalist Gideon Lincecum, who opined that "it would require a snug little volume to do justice to the harvester ants" (Burkhalter 1965). He was right, but this isn't it. The snug little volume is in my drawer where it will presumably stay.

Nevertheless, here are the harvester ants as they appear in mythology, in literature, and in science. Some of the imaginative literature, which evolved into "fact" over time, now provides a little humor in the midst of a vast and otherwise serious entomological record. My primary concern herein is a summary of those serious publications in natural history, biogeography, and species identification as well as my own findings, mostly in the area of evolution. Evolution, or "descent with modification," was a controversial topic long before Darwin, but the accumulated evidence for life's history has now become so irresistible that the pope has given the theory his blessing (Holden 1996). Darwin's bulldog, T. H. Huxley, described the study of evolution as "retrospective prophecy" (Berry 1923). I view evolutionary study as a kind of historical natural history.

Many individuals and institutions contributed to this ten-year project. Foremost of these is Roy R. Snelling of the Los Angeles County Natural History Museum, who provided almost all of the South American and Caribbean species. A new species of harvester appears here, named for Snelling, its discoverer. For additional specimens I thank Axel O. Bachmann (Museo Argentino de Ciencias Naturales "Bernardino Rivadavia," Buenos Aires, Argentina), Carlos Roberto F. Brandão (Museu de Zoologia da Universidade de São Paulo, São Paulo, Brazil), the late Frank M. Carpenter (Museum of Comparative Zoology, Harvard University, Cambridge, Massachusetts), James C. Cokendolpher (Entomology Department, Texas Tech University, Lubbock), Stefan P. Cover (Museum of Comparative Zoology, Harvard University), Erich Diller (Zoologische Staatssammlung, München, Germany), Oscar F. Francke (Department of Biological Sciences, Texas Tech University), Robert Johnson (Department of Botany, Arizona State University, Tempe), William P. MacKay (Department of Entomology, Texas A&M University, College Station), Sanford D. Porter (Department of Biological Science, Florida State University, Tallahassee), Steven O. Shattuck (R. M. Bohart Museum of Entomology, University of California, Davis), Zine D. Ajmat de Toledo (Fundación Miguel Lillo, San Miguel de Tucumán, Tucumán, Argentina), and Edward O. Wilson (Museum of Comparative Zoology, Harvard University). The institutional affiliations listed here are those at the time of original correspondence.

Information, comments, and suggestions are also appreciated from Paul E. Blom and William H. Clark (Orma J. Smith Museum of Natural History, Albertson College of Idaho, Caldwell), Barry Bolton (British Museum [Natural History], London), Deborah M. Gordon (Department of Biological Sciences, Stanford University, Stanford, California), William P. MacKay, Frank Merickel (Department of Plant, Soil, and Entomological Sciences; University of Idaho, Moscow), Mark W. Moffett (Museum of Comparative Zoology, Harvard University), and Jeanette N. Wheeler and the late George C. Wheeler (accomplished myrmecologists, San Antonio, Texas).

Special thanks go to Arthur C. Cole (Professor Emeritus, Department of Zoology, University of Tennessee, Knoxville), who wished me luck in this endeavor. Much of the stimulus for this work was provided by Dr. Cole's 1968 book on the North American harvester ants, and many of the maps in this book are based upon that University of Tennessee Press publication. While still very young, I used it to identify a large, brick-red "bug" on the playgrounds of College Station, Texas. It was *Pogonomyrmex barbatus,* the red harvester ant, the first insect that I identified to species. Years later, and only after completing a study of the chromosome numbers of the harvester ants, I came across the records of some questions that Cole (1963) entertained at an international meeting in Italy. He was asked if anyone had looked at the chromosome numbers of the harvesters. Cole replied that it had not been done, but "maybe somebody will be encouraged to take it up."

Even now many harvester ants are known from little more than their dead and dried bodies. Perhaps someone will be encouraged to fill in these remaining gaps as well.

The World of the Harvester Ants

Chapter 1

Introduction

"What will the people eat?" asked the spirits. "Let corn be discovered." And no sooner had the command been given than Quetzalcoatl noticed a red ant carrying a kernel of true corn.

"Where did you find it?" he asked. But she would not answer him. Again and again he questioned her, until at last she said, "Follow me."

Then Quetzalcoatl changed into a black ant and followed the red ant to the edge of a mountain. This was Food Mountain, where corn, beans, peppers, and all the other foods had been hidden since the beginning of the world. "Come this way," she said, and she entered a tunnel that led inside.

With the help of the red ant, the black ant dragged corn kernels back to the spirit place, where the other spirits were waiting. When the corn arrived, the spirits chewed it for us and placed it on our lips. In this way we were made strong.

"Now, what will we do with Food Mountain?" asked Quetzalcoatl.

"We will crack it open, so the people can have all the food," said the other spirits.

As they talked, the one called Nanahuatl split the mountain and revealed what was inside. But the rain was jealous, and he and his children rushed in and stole the food before the other spirits could give it to the people. Corn, beans, peppers, sage, everything was stolen.

The rain spirits still have the food that was in Food Mountain. They give back only a part of it each year— and some years less than others—in exchange for human blood.

—JOHN BIERHORST,
THE HUNGRY WOMAN:
MYTHS AND LEGENDS OF THE AZTECS

There are many ants worldwide that can be described as harvesters because they collect, store, and eat seeds (figs. 1.1, 1.2). The subject of this book is more limited. I consider only the New World ants of the genera *Pogonomyrmex* and *Ephebomyrmex,* because in the United States at least, this is what one normally means by "harvester ant." There are sixty living species in these two genera, found from southern Canada to Tierra del Fuego near the tip of South America. The most conspicuous and famous ants in North America are indeed the large, reddish harvesters of the western plains and deserts, which build huge, populous mounds and attack intruders like a pack of tiny red dogs (figs. 1.3, 1.4, 1.5). These plains harvesters (and the horned lizard, which eats them) were first reported by members of the Long expedition to the Rocky Mountains, in 1820 (Evans 1997).

1.1 The Comanche harvester ant (Pogonomyrmex comanche) *of central Texas. This worker is standing on a sunflower seed.*

1.2 The Comanche harvester ant in dorsal view.

1.3 The huge mound of the western harvester ant (Pogonomyrmex occidentalis).

Among their many common names are red ant, stinging ant, agricultural ant, mound-building ant, and a few more in German, Spanish, and Native American. Scientific names are always latinized and their origins are often obvious, but even here misnomers confuse the issue (see appendix 1). The scientific names do provide some useful generalizations and a starting point for this presentation.

Most species are members of the genus *Pogonomyrmex*. This

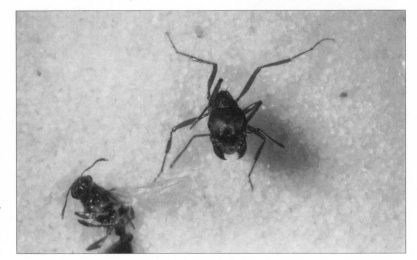

1.4 A defensive Comanche forager stares up into the camera, its jaws agape. It has captured a fire ant queen, seen to the left.

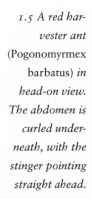

1.5 A red harvester ant (Pogonomyrmex barbatus) in head-on view. The abdomen is curled underneath, with the stinger pointing straight ahead.

name means "bearded ant" due to the whiskers found on the lower surface of the head of some, but not all, "pogos" (fig. 1.6). Many early naturalists believed worker ants (the familiar kind, those without wings) to be males, perhaps because of their intense activity outside the nest and because of their aggressive behavior. The beard must have seemed a clincher, but those naturalists were wrong. All worker ants are actually females. Males can't sting, don't work, rarely appear above ground, and have wings but no functional beard. They mate and die. A few dissections under a microscope would presumably have revealed the truth to Buckley, Lincecum, and many other writers of the nineteenth century: the stinger itself is a modified egg-laying organ which has lost that function. Even modern texts on insect-related allergies sometimes describe the stinging behavior using masculine pronouns.

The harvester's painful sting has been ranked in scientific publications as worse than all but a few North American insects (Schmidt 1989). The huge purple-orange tarantula wasps and the

1.6 A queen of the desert harvester ant (Pogonomyrmex desertorum). It removed its wings after mating. The large thorax contains the flight muscles, and the beard is visible beneath the head.

fuzzy, wingless "cow killer" wasps, or "velvet ants," are said to hurt even more, but their stings are only acutely painful, whereas the harvester's effects linger for a day or more. The "bite" of the greatly feared imported fire ant is likewise a sting, but it is a mere pin prick compared to that of the common, native red harvester (see Vinson 1997 for a good summary of fire ant biology). When a character in a Western movie is staked out over an ant mound, the victim is probably being offered to the harvester. Those of us who have been stung by several ants at a time while excavating nests can hardly imagine the excruciating death delivered by thousands of angry harvesters.

If any of the indigenous North American peoples really did use harvesters for torture, the Aztecs would likely be among that number. A more wholesome role for the ant is certainly provided by their creation myths, and these are doubly interesting because they appear to contain the earliest references to *Pogonomyrmex*. The Aztecs credit these insects with the gift of corn or maize to humanity, and it would be hard to imagine a more important aspect of American Indian culture. The red ant in the above Aztec legend appears to be the Mexican, or red, harvester ant, *Pogonomyrmex barbatus*. The Food Mountain would then be the gravel mound in which food, including corn grains, is stored. This legend might be two thousand years old. (See the National Public Radio cassette, *Stories from the Spirit World: The Legend of the Sun.*)

Harvester ants also play a major role in the mythology of the Navaho. The general name for these cursed creatures is *wóde' ecahi· coh* (big pinching ant), and the chant complex known as the Red Antway is performed to propitiate the insects when they have been offended by disturbances to their mound (Wyman and Bailey 1964; Wyman 1965). The ritual can last for days and includes dances and special meals. Offenses against the ants include urinating, spitting, walking, or sleeping on an anthill (as well as digging it up, burning it, etc.).

Chiricahua Apache children who choose to sleep on the mounds will join the ranks of the self-taught, but children are taught by others not to urinate on the mounds (Opler 1965). The alleged counterattack by the ant is much worse than mere stings. The wicked ants supposedly shoot little rocks into the offender's urinary tract!

Acoma Indians used these warlike qualities of the harvesters to their own ends. Their chiefs carried anthill gravel in a pouch, and Acoma warriors left scalps on anthills for days, asking the ants to kill the remains. Their prayers were always answered. And the Zuni Indians say that, whenever an enemy falls, an anthill is formed (Wyman 1965).

The Apache had an interesting method for curing the sting of the red ant. A person insensitive to the sting rubbed dirt on the wound and said, "Now this person is just like me. Leave him alone. Go away. I'm watching him." It is not clear what is meant by "insensitive." The sting is excruciatingly painful to seemingly everyone.

The Navaho warn us that ants should not be swallowed in either food or drink, and the natural enemy of harvesters is part of the treatment when these warnings go unheeded: a horned lizard is dipped in water and the liquid is consumed by the offender. Horned lizards themselves do not mind offending the ants—they have been known to sit by a nest and lap up all comers and goers until the nest is practically empty, as they have a substance in their blood that protects them against the venom of the harvester ant. If the Navaho must destroy a nest, there is a plant called "red ant killer" that is used in a solution poured onto the mound. Goshute Indians ate some insects, but not the western harvester because of its strong taste (Chamberlin 1908).

Where did the harvesters come from? One answer comes from the Navaho and one from a very different source, Western science.

In Navaho mythology, the murderous Ant Peoples originated in the underworld but later emerged to settle on the surface of the earth (Wyman 1965). In the process, Horned Toad swallowed their weapons and became immune to the red ants and to lightning. Its chemical armor against ants has now been confirmed, but it probably offers no protection from the thunderbolt.

A scientific view of harvester origins will be presented in the chapter on evolution and biogeography, the area of my own research. They probably came on the scene about sixty million years ago in the northern part of South America, evolving from predatory forest dwellers. Their presence in the southwestern deserts of the United States is due to a long northward migration. Some of these migrants were whisked into the Caribbean on board a gigantic east-bound rock now known as Hispaniola.

Harvester ants have appeared in epic poems and novels too. In Milton's *Paradise Lost,* the first insect to rise from the earth during creation is an Old World species of harvester ant, the kind mentioned in the Bible in Proverbs VI, verse six, as a model of industry. The Canadian author Frederick Grove (1947) wrote an epic account of an expedition of tropical, anthropomorphic leaf-cutter ants that encounter the western harvester on their journey into northern lands. The pogos are considered civilized and interesting, though formidable enemies. The commander of their armies is Minna-ca, who asks the fungus-growing leaf-cutters about the shape of the earth, day and night, the seasons, and the inclination of the earth's axis. A parley ensues in which the leaf-cutters enter the huge harvester nest on its southern slope, noting the cleared disk of earth, the pebble mound, and the stored seeds. After the tropical explorers leave this nest, they encounter one *Pogonomyrmex* colony after another, fighting each one along the way (fig. 1.7).

There are fiction books for children about harvesters too. Darling's book (1977) and that of Dorros (1987) are recommended. Darling's book relates the adventures of a harvester and its pet cricket. This is endearing fiction, but it is based on fact. Large ant nests really do harbor strange guests, and these include very small crickets and beetles, which ride about on the backs of their hosts.

I have come to the end of this introduction, which has set the stage for a book on natural history. The rest of what I have to relate is the result of fieldwork and laboratory investigation, and much of it was done by a former denizen of the very zoology de-

1.7 The nest entrance of the rough harvester ant (Pogono-myrmex ru-gosus) being investigated by some passing workers of the smaller, lighter-colored California harvester (P. californicus).

partment in which I am writing these words. It was accomplished over the course of thirty-seven years by the polymath William Morton Wheeler. I would like to tell you that he came here in 1899 with one burning desire—to study the harvester ants of Texas. Unfortunately, this isn't the case. When he arrived from the East he found so little laboratory equipment that he was unable to do his intended research. While pondering his problems one day along Austin's famous Barton Creek, he spied a leaf-cutter ant and its tender green cargo. Could he study leaf-cutters without too much equipment? Yes, he could and did. Wheeler studied the harvester ants too, up until the time of his death from a heart attack (Mallis 1971). During the course of his investigations Wheeler discovered and named nine harvester ant species. This is the record and it won't be broken. The Austin area does in fact contain the type localities of both *Pogonomyrmex comanche* (fig. 1.8) and *Ephebomyrmex imberbiculus.*

Wheeler's portrait is hanging in the hall of Patterson Laboratories at the University of Texas (similar to fig. 1.9), and as I passed beneath it I sometimes wondered how he would have received this effort, for he was a severe critic and my findings are often contrary to his own. He once wrote an article with the express purpose of attacking a geologist who studied harvester ants on the side (Wheeler 1902c). It still seems strange to me that this erudite biologist studied ants, for the English philosopher Alfred North

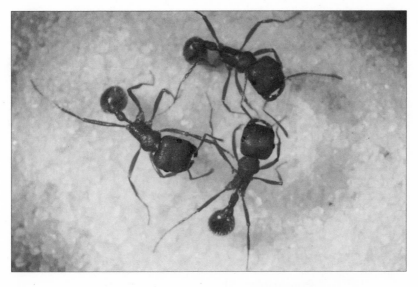

1.8 *A trio of communicating Comanche harvesters.*

Whitehead once said that Wheeler was the only living person who could have conversed comfortably with Aristotle. His mastery of foreign dialects was so great that he could even laugh in several languages (or so it was said).

1.9 *William Morton Wheeler as a professor at the University of Texas in 1903.* (Cactus Yearbook, CN #09207, Center for American History, University of Texas at Austin. Courtesy of Texas Student Publications.)

Wheeler's work and that of hundreds of others is summarized in these few pages. I hope the reader finds some useful information and a little entertainment too.

A few words about this book. I wrote this book for both the interested, educated lay reader and the ant specialist. Therefore, some items of technical detail are included but have been largely relegated to the appendixes. Also, the reader will find a section of illustrations that contains line drawings, along with distribution maps, for all of the species. Legs and antennae have little identification value in these drawings; thus, they have been pruned. Sometimes appendages are missing, as in rare and ancient type specimens. These drawings are listed in alphabetical order with the exception of *Hylomyrma reitteri*. This South American species is not a harvester and appears at the end of that section.

Chapter 2
The Home of the Harvester Ants

. . . that malignant universe of mounds.

—H. P. LOVECRAFT,
THE LURKING FEAR

The Land of the Harvester Ants

Looking at all sixty species and at the distribution map, one could generalize that harvester ants live in grasslands, in deserts, in forests, and on mountains to an elevation of almost three miles (fig. 2.1). A glance at the individual distribution maps will show that grasslands and deserts are really more typical, and this should be no surprise because grass seeds are among the ants' favorite foods. It is even more generally true that harvesters are confined to arid lands, whatever the landform or predominant vegetation. In North and South America this normally means the western half of the continent, where the coastal mountain ranges have produced a dry area called a rainshadow and semiarid plains and pampas nearby.

The two most commonly collected species illustrate this state of affairs. The western harvester *(Pogonomyrmex occidentalis)* and the red harvester *(P. barbatus)* are typical in the sense that they prefer only moderately arid lands—a sort of middle ground for

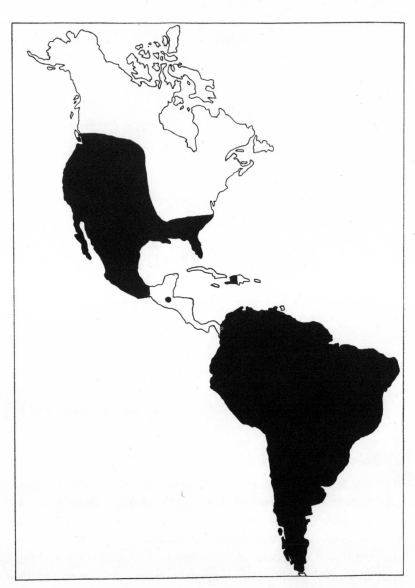

the genus (Moody and Francke 1982). Their nests are scattered across the vast central and western grasslands of the United States, but neither species is found in the hottest habitats, nor are they found at the other extreme among moist vegetation, as are a few of the South American ants. Other harvesters can handle more desert heat than these two. The champions in North America are probably the California harvester *(P. californicus)* and *P. magnacanthus,* which I christen here as the "big-eyed harvester" because of its outsized compound eyes; the eyes alone are sufficient to identify the species. The California ant forages for seeds in temperatures up to 130°F and can be found outside the nest at 140°F, although they climb up into the vegetation above such hot soils (Whitford and Ettershank 1975). No one has made similar measurements for *P. magnacanthus.* I collected both species in early summer in the Mojave Desert when the blazing white sands of Indio, California, were too hot to touch, and their presence in Death Valley underlines their tolerance of infernal temperatures.

At the opposite extreme in North America is the Florida harvester *(P. badius),* which is confined to the eastern United States where there are no deserts. But even here the preference remains for dry sandy areas. The ant will not nest in shade (Carlson and Gentry 1973).

Two species are unusual because they are strongly tied to the forest. These are *P. montanus* and *P. comanche,* which I call the montane and Comanche harvester, respectively. Much is known about *P. montanus* because its discoverer, Dr. William MacKay, is an ecologist. This ant is confined to montane piney woods in California where it seems to be occupying a marginal habitat (MacKay 1981). Living there is pushing the limits for its kind. The shallow nests, lack of seed storage, and an unusually high colony extinction rate suggest that this move into the higher forests was a risky maneuver.

Our knowledge about the other forester, the Comanche ant, is paradoxically nil. Paradoxically because of its central range, because of its occurrence between the University of Texas and the huge agricultural school in College Station, and because William Morton Wheeler was its discoverer. Nothing about its biology has been previously published, with the exception of a mating swarm observation (Strandtmann 1942). (I have been observing several nests in Bastrop State Park, and I will report on my findings in subsequent chapters.) This harvester seems tied to scattered islands of sandy post-oak forest, with a mixture of pines, such as the loblolly. It might be a relict, hanging on to bits and pieces of a habitat that is slowly vanishing as the grasslands encroach.

One South American harvester lives high in the Andes at an elevation of 14,000 feet, almost 3 miles up (Kusnezov 1951, 1952). This is *P. longibarbis,* the long-bearded harvester. No other species lives at this altitude. Several ants inhabit the mild eastern grasslands of the pampas. Most of the others are found between these two geographical icons in deserts both hot and cold. The most tolerant harvester of all might be one of these South Americans, *Ephebomyrmex cunicularius* (fig. 2.2) (Kusnezov 1951, 1953). The name means "youthful ant that digs in the ground." The juvenile attribute is its lack of a beard. Its habitats range from areas with copious summer rains to dry savannas, even to the extremes of hot deserts. It also lives in the mountains but is yet a flatlander compared to *P. longibarbis*. Until now *E. cunicularius* was thought to be a pogo, but the evolutionary tree (see chapter 6) reveals that it is actually a member of the lesser known genus, *Ephebomyrmex*. Why did this fact escape Wheeler and especially the South American myrmecologists for a hundred years? Perhaps its large size and rapid movements placed it among the pogos, for they are the giants and the sprinters of the two harvester ant genera.

Where Harvesters Build Their Nests

It is difficult to generalize when the subject deals with sixty species spanning two continents, but one thing is universally true of the harvesters—they nest in the ground (fig. 2.3). Many ants do not. Some ants build their nests in trees, in the walls of buildings, in rolled-up leaves, in bits and pieces of this and that, and so on. The only exceptions to the fossorial habits of harvesters are the few

2.2 Ephebo-
myrmex
cunicularius *of
South America.
Formerly
thought to be a
pogo, this ant
has a broad
taste in habitat.*

reports of nests in rocks, and these species are known to nest in soil too.

A nest begins when a recently mated winged female (a queen) discovers a patch of soil suitable for tunneling. She is all alone at this time and the small chamber of the incipient nest will be enlarged by her offspring during the years to come. Favored sites vary somewhat and depend upon the species. The well-studied red harvester provides a convenient example because of its broad tastes. Nests are found under rocks, at the bases of trees, in fields and other open areas, in cultivated groves, in asphalt cracks, and along sidewalks, streets, and highways. A study at Texas Tech University found 94 percent of the nests in open areas (Moody and Francke 1982).

This species has soil preferences too. It prefers clay loam on roughly level ground and avoids pure sand even though many other harvesters prefer or require it. The western harvester prefers similar soils, but it sometimes builds its nests on vertical cliffs, and it is now expanding its range in drought-afflicted areas of North Dakota by following ditches along the sides of roads (DeMers 1993). Western harvester ants have an instinct to build their mound on level ground by dropping gravel around the nest entrance, but when the entrance happens to be on a vertical surface, the insect appears to be disturbed when the gravel plummets out of sight (Wheeler and Wheeler 1963).

Harvesters are as agrarian as their name implies and few species will be found within human city limits. However, the red harvester is a city dweller on both the northern and southern extremes of its range, being found on the streets of Lubbock, Texas, and Mexico City. The western, like the red, is also an exception, and I have seen its colonies in the streets of Denver, Colorado. The rough harvester ant *(P. rugosus)* is a close relative of the red and western species and it sometimes builds its nests in limestone so hard that a backhoe can't break into it (Whitford, Johnson, and Ramirez 1976). The Florida harvester and the California harvester have very different requirements; the former requires sandy soil and the latter prefers it. The Florida harvester can be found on sand dunes and among the palmettoes (Hutchins 1958).

Nesting conditions can be quite different in South America. The ancient Southern Beech forests on the slopes of the Andes are home to several species that build their nests under the cover of leaf litter, stones, and pieces of wood (Kusnezov 1951). In this part of the world, one often finds volcanic ash within the nest. Moist clay is an odd preference, but that is where you will find *P. lobatus,* which dwells lower down, in the humid river valleys of Argentina, Brazil, and Uruguay (Bruch 1923). Both Caribbean species, *E. saucius* and *E. schmitti,* live on the island of Hispaniola, where they nest among stones and cacti in rubble-strewn desert (Wheeler and Mann 1914).

Some of the most unusual sites were reported for species that are known from only one or a few nests. *Pogonomyrmex anzensis* (fig. 2.4) is known from a single encounter in the 1950s in Anza Desert State Park of southern California, and its nest was under a boulder (Snelling and George 1979). I went to the type locality and was unable to find this elusive harvester. Stranger still is the earliest reported nest of *Ephebomyrmex abdominalis* (fig. 2.5), which was found not under but *inside* a rock (Gallardo 1932). Sometimes the nest site can be described as unnatural—*P. guatemaltecus* was found living in the sand piles left behind by railroad cars (Wheeler 1914).

The Ins and Outs of the Harvester Nest

Harvester ant nests are usually systems of subterranean tunnels and galleries, but sometimes part of the nest occupies a dome of earth and gravel that the ants themselves build up from excavated

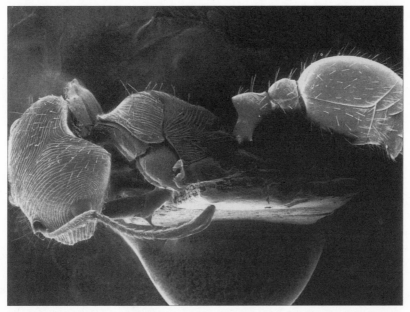

2.4 *A worker of the Anza Desert harvester,* Pogonomyrmex anzensis, *(scanning electron micrograph). The species is known from a single nest discovered in the 1950s.*

2.5 *The winged female or queen of the rarely collected* Ephebomyrmex abdominalis *of South America. This is a type specimen.*

materials and from surface scrapings nearby. These mounds are the hallmark of the western harvester and are common for the red and for the rough. The western ant has the most complex nest of all sixty species and is a useful model for an explanation of mound anatomy.

The largest gravel-covered mound on record was 3 feet high

and 16 feet wide (Schmidt, Schmidt, and Snelling 1986). Such nests can be 20 feet deep, presumably stopping when they reach the water table or impenetrable rock. The mound is in the center of a flat clearing, which can be 50 feet wide (Gilbert 1960). There are between one and eleven entrances, typically on the southeast side of the mound, and they will be found several inches up from ground level (Cole 1934a). The mound and the soil beneath it are riddled with tunnels and chambers, which function as seed storage bins (granaries), nurseries, and garbage areas. When the garbage areas are filled, these rooms are sealed off from the rest of the nest. Some species undertake a spring cleaning, which produces a pulse of waste that is carried to the outside trash heaps at the edge of the clearing (Gentry and Stiritz 1972). Tunnels are up to half an inch wide and chambers can be 6 inches long. Up to 150 chambers have been counted in a single nest, and these are plastered with salivary juices by at least some North American harvesters and Marcus's harvester *(P. marcusi)* (fig. 2.6) of Bolivia (McCook 1879; Marcus 1953). Flowers are placed around the juveniles of several species, but these are probably more for humidity control than for looks (MacKay 1981). When repairs are needed, seeds and brood are moved from the damaged areas to safer parts of the nest.

Western harvester mounds are covered with gravel, plant matter, fossils, gold dust, broken glass, nails, locomotive cinders, vol-

2.6 Marcus's harvester of Bolivia. (Pogonomyrmex marcusi).

canic ash, charcoal, and semiprecious stones. The material coating the mound is cemented together with a secretion from the mouth of the ants and is then packed down by tiny legs. This exterior "rind" is waterproofing. If the nest does become waterlogged, workers allow it to dry faster by boring holes in the surface. If the mound is damaged, workers will repair the nest before they will collect food (Taylor 1978).

Foraging ants travel on or off trails, but these are usually pre-existing types—cattle trails, clearings, and so forth. However, the red harvester and the rough harvester make their own trails. Some "trunk trails," the widest trails, are blazed to a width of 2 inches or more.

The functions of tunnels, chambers, and foraging trails are obvious enough, but what about the mounds themselves and the huge clearings that surround them? Their functions remain controversial. There has been no shortage of ideas about these over the last hundred years. The mound is supposedly an incubator for brood or a high-ground refuge during floods. Floods are certainly a threat. During the great Texas torrent of 1875, masses of red harvesters were seen floating away on the waters (Mitchell and Pierce 1912).

The clearing has provoked more than just two hypotheses. Depending upon the author, this open area is a firebreak, a dehumidifier, a heat absorber, a target for flying males from other nests seeking mates, or a drying surface for seeds and brood. There is a report of one gallon of seeds drying on the clearing of a red harvester mound (Lincecum 1874). Wet brood are also put out to dry. Perhaps the open area makes it easier for foraging workers to move about quickly. Also, because no plants are allowed to grow there, it prevents roots from destroying the tunnels and chambers below (Wu 1990). Plants would also provide unwelcome shade for the nest and would compete for soil moisture. The rough harvester defoliates and kills plants that grow too close to the nest (Rissing 1988).

Perhaps protection from enemies is the function of the clearing. Such predators as horned toads can't hide in plain sight. The Florida harvester often covers the whole clearing with charcoal, a material used to adsorb (pick up) chemicals. The black coating would retain the harvester chemical territorial markers more efficiently than soil and would be a deterrent to other ants that might approach the nest (Gordon 1984a). Red harvesters are serious about this area, whatever its function might be. Even cow droppings are not suffered to grace the clearing (Lincecum 1866). The ants take them apart bit by bit until nothing remains. One author believed that buffalo wallows originated from the huge clearings of western harvesters (Nagel 1969).

All other harvester ant nests are simpler than this. Mayr's harvester *(Ephebomyrmex mayri)* (figs. 2.7, 2.8) of northern Colombia is the strangest looking of all sixty species, and it has one of the simplest homes (Kugler 1978, 1984; Kugler and Hincapie 1983). It builds no mound or clearing, and its single entrance is hidden beneath stones or leaves. The total depth is a mere 6 inches. There are but two levels and just a few chambers. Looking for *mayri* can be confusing because it moves its nest several times a year. This could be an advantage of a simple home. A moving target isn't a reliable source of food for predators.

Between these two extremes of complex and simple are nests like those of the California harvester. They are typically marked by a bowl-shaped crater instead of a dome-shaped mound. The crater is up to 2 feet wide and 2 inches deep. The entrance is in the middle or just off-center, and visible at some distance is the ring of chaff (discarded hulls of seeds), which looks like a golden halo about the whole edifice. Sometimes the nest superstructure is a mound up to 12 feet wide instead of a crater, or it is little more than a hole in the ground. Unlike the western harvester, the Cali-

2.7 *The strangest harvester of all is Mayr's harvester of Colombia. Its black, velvety appearance is unique, and that trait prompted others to place the species in its own subgenus* (Forelomyrmex).

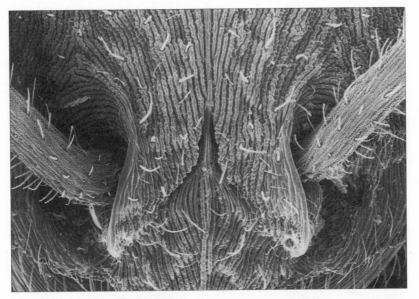

2.8 *The heavily wrinkled exoskeleton between the antennae of Mayr's harvester is highlighted by this scanning electron micrograph.*

fornia species seldom clears plants from the area surrounding its nest and does not make or use foraging trails (Essig 1929; Wheeler and Wheeler 1973).

Some anthills are ephemeral—here one moment and gone the next. *Pogonomyrmex laticeps* dwells high in the mountains of Argentina, where Nicholas Kusnezov watched its craters disappear as they were spirited away by sudden gusts of the Andean wind (1951).

Locking the Door and Making the Move

A few harvesters close the nest regularly at night. Some close it irregularly and as a result of various stimuli. They will also pick up and leave the old nest for a new one nearby that has been abandoned, or they will build a new one from scratch. Nest closure is an answer to immediate danger, night, winter, storms, heat, poisons, dry spells, and rain. Red harvesters plug the nest entrance against a rainstorm with their own bodies (Lincecum 1866). It is also typical for ant queens to plug up their little incipient nest until they have a chance to raise some young (Wildermuth and Davis 1931).

The nest is closed each evening around sunset by the Florida harvester, the California, the western, and the Comanche. The actions of the Florida harvester serve as an example of these proceedings. Several workers cooperate to close the nest with pebbles, sand, and even vegetation. They kick sand backwards into the hole like little dogs trying to bury a bone. The whole process takes about an hour and leaves from one to several ants outside for the night (Turner 1909). These lurk nearby until the nest opens around sunrise. Western harvesters use some kind of oral secretion to cement the temporary portal into place (McCook 1882). Nest closing by the Comanches was unknown until recently. It proceeds much like that of the Florida harvester, right down to the sand kicking. Sometimes the portal is closed so well that the clearing looks unoccupied, but I have also seen little pyramids about half an inch high marking the hidden entrance (figs. 2.9, 2.10). One or two workers remain outside and occasionally crawl up into the weeds where they hide until morning.

Danger lurking nearby can provoke nest closure. Widow spiders seem to provoke this response—as well as a change in the location of the entrance—in the Florida and rough harvesters (Hölldobler 1970; MacKay and MacKay 1984). The western harvester lives in a colder clime than the Florida ant, so it closes its nests for the winter, as do the California harvester and, according to some authors, *P. salinus*.

A behavior somewhat akin to nest plugging is used to deal with bothersome creatures and noxious substances. It also provides some comic relief to the naturalist. The red harvester fills in the tiny nests of nearby ants with soil, but it adds insult to injury

2.9 This photo was taken at midnight when the Comanche nest was closed for the evening. The two specks on the clearing are workers that will stay outside until morning.

2.10 This photo was taken while the Comanche nest of the previous figure was being opened at first light. The dark spot on the clearing is the nest entrance, surrounded by a small pile of soil left over from the plug.

when it uses earthworm feces instead (Lincecum 1866). It also fills the pits of ant-lions, which are creatures with jaws like ice tongs that skewer unwary ants unlucky enough to tumble into their pits (fig. 2.11).

Insecticides on the nest clearing are greeted with a coating of soil brought up from the depths of the nest and spread over the poison to absorb it (Warnhoff 1947). Surprisingly, the western harvester also fills miscellaneous objects, such as mollusk shells and hoofprints, which it fills in with leaves (King 1963).

Ants sometimes leave home when it gets too hot, either during the dry season or when other creatures threaten. The ramblings of sheep can cause the western harvester to clear out, as can nest damage, nest desiccation, and poisons offered by humans. One nest was found underwater a year after it was abandoned. Sometimes they move into an old, empty nest, but they often build a new one. They typically follow foraging trails during emigration, and refugee columns half a mile long have been reported (McCook 1882). A shaded nest is also enough to make the Florida harvester leave home for good. They scurry to a new site up to 30 feet away with their jaws full of juveniles and seeds.

Emigrations are made in the spring and fall with no obvious stimulus (Harvester ant migrations 1970). There are few records of red harvester emigrations. In one case they tolerated a blacksmith's fireplace overhead (McCook 1877). But on another occasion, rough harvesters provoked a move that was followed by yet another when the red ants found themselves next to their own species in the new location (Hölldobler 1976a).

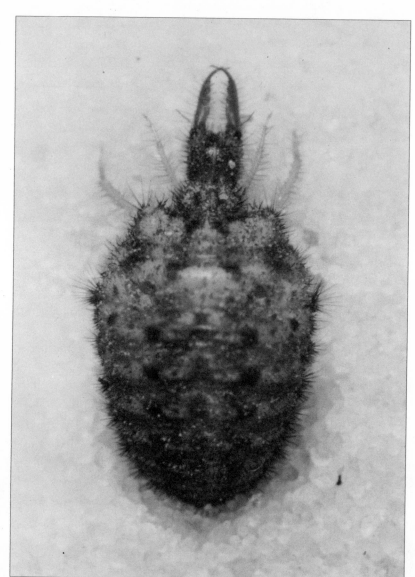

2.11 An ant-lion, which traps and devours harvesters. This larval stage lives in pits in the sand. The adult has wings and looks like a small, clumsy dragonfly.

When red harvesters move they take their garbage as well (Hölldobler and Wilson 1990). The California and Maricopa harvesters and *P. salinus* move occasionally but not always wisely. The latter species once moved from a safe area to an area that had been treated with insecticide (Crowell 1963). Surprisingly, no one has ever reported an emigration of the widely distributed and greatly studied rough harvester ant.

The South American record is predictably scanty. Mayr's harvester is known to emigrate frequently, as often as once a month. They do it the easy way by occupying an abandoned nest instead of building a new one. Some take it even easier—they are carried by their nestmates to the new location (Kugler and Hincapie 1983). William Morton Wheeler saw something similar, which he interpreted as a form of play—clusters of red harvesters that were attached to one another by their jaws (1910).

Chapter 3
Living and Eating in the Nest

The harvesters are in the corn! Kara! Kara!
— THE EPIC OF ISHTAR
AND IZDUBAR

The City Is a Family

The harvester ant mound is a giant single-parent family committed to the care of sisters and an occasional brother (fig. 3.1). A family of ten thousand, like that of the western harvester, achieves city status under a single roof. The single parent is both mother and queen of the realm. The males die after mating and the queen must go it alone (fig. 3.2). The children can be either full or half siblings because the queen commonly mates with five or six different males (but only once with each male), with the result being that her children can have different fathers (Hölldobler 1976a). Nests are usually begun by such a single queen, but occasionally several newly mated females cooperate in the digging before all but one are ousted. It is typical for only one ruler to reign over the growing family.

Adult sister populations of a few dozen to a few hundred are typical of *Ephebomyrmex* nests in general and of quite a few South American pogos (Kusnezov 1951). Some South American species

3.1 California harvesters tending brood. The larvae of ants are maggotlike, with translucent skin. One is lying on its back near the bottom of the photo.

have populations approaching 1,000. For example, here is the complete census from the largest nest of Marcus's harvester ever found in Bolivia: 619 adult workers, 20 callows (newly molted ants), 101 pupae, 87 larvae, and 45 eggs. No queen was found in this city, and there were no adult males or virgin queens (winged reproductive females that haven't mated) present at the time (Marcus and Marcus 1951; Marcus 1953).

3.2 These two desert harvesters were caught in 1981 during the mating ritual, and they remain locked in position. The male is the darker and smaller of the two.

The whopper of all sixty harvesters is *P. coarctatus* of Argentina at over half an inch, but head counts never exceed six hundred. The situation is different in North America where big ants tend to have big colonies of several thousand workers. For example, the red harvester of Texas, which is much smaller than *P. coarctatus,* can have an extended family of more than twelve thousand sisters (Wildermuth and Davis 1931). Numbers like this are also typical of the Florida, western, and rough harvesters, as well as *P. salinus* and *P. subnitidus.* It's not clear which insect holds the record for the largest metropolis, but it would be fitting if it were held by a red harvester family living within the limits of Mexico City.

The consistently smallest towns are those of *P. laticeps* of the high Andes (Kusnezov 1951). Some tiny *Ephebomyrmex* might be expected to hold the record (*Ephebomyrmex* colonies tend to be smaller than pogo colonies), and that is probably true when it comes to the smallest population ever censused. However, the Andean ant lives in a marginal habitat and its normal population of fifty or less reflects that perilous condition, much like that of the montane harvester of California.

Mixed nests are those that contain not just one but two species of ants. The rough and the red harvesters are known to room together as well as with the social parasites *P. anergismus* (which lives with the rough harvester and the red [Cole 1968]) and *P. colei* (which lives only with the rough [Rissing 1983]). (Social parasites are ants with no worker caste that live in the nest of a different species.) There might well be a nest with three species out there somewhere: the rough, the red, and one of the parasites.

How is it that a city populated almost entirely by a sterile worker caste came about in the first place? After all, about 99 percent of a colony consists of sisters who raise their mother's children instead of their own. It would seem that natural selection would weed out individuals like this, ants that never reproduce, leaving only queens and males in the mound—everything *but* workers. Darwin himself worried about this and thought it might be a fatal flaw in his evolutionary theory. However, the theory explains the enigma.

This summary focuses on the female—because all workers are females and the concern here is with their origin and maintenance—and on monogamous mating as the simplest case. The sterile condition of the modern harvester worker is an example of an end point in this particular evolutionary process. Many other stinging insects show variability in the evolution of a sterile worker caste. Male harvesters develop from unfertilized eggs and thus have only half the number of chromosomes that their sisters, mothers, and any other females have. This throws a monkey wrench into the whole problem of determining the genetic closeness of relationships within the mound (Seger 1996). First, like human daughters, daughters of an ant couple get half of their chromosomes from their mother, the other half from their father. Unlike human fathers, however, father ants have only one set of chromosomes, so each daughter gets a copy of that entire set (male ants don't have sons or fathers because males develop from unfertilized eggs). Therefore, human sisters are only 50 percent related to one another because that is the likelihood of sharing copies of the same set of genes. Ant sisters are 75 percent related to one another because they get an identical chromosome set from their haploid father while getting copies of the same chromosomes from the queen only half the time (fig. 3.3) (Oster and Wilson 1978). But like humans, they would be only 50 percent related to their own offspring if they reproduced sexually by mating with a male. In

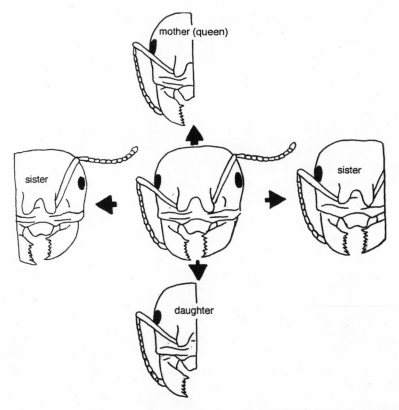

3.3 Worker harvester ants do not have offspring. Only their mother lays viable eggs. Worker daughter is hypothetical.

other words, the genes of the workers would seem to be represented better in the next generation if they raise future queens and sterile sisters (with whom they share 75 percent of their genes) through another breeder (mom) instead of bearing their own daughters (with whom they would share only 50 percent of their genes).

Most biologists learn the above as the "reason" for the existence of a sterile worker caste. There is a problem, however. The workers are indeed more closely related to their sisters than to any daughter they might have if they could reproduce, but they are more distantly related to brothers (the queen's sons) than they would be to their own sons (only 25 percent compared to 50 percent). The *average* relatedness to the two sexes is therefore the same in either scenario. A recent review of this problem began with a warning that "this apparently simple question is among the most difficult in population genetics" (Maynard Smith and Szathmáry 1995).

However this sterile worker caste came about, it seems that natural selection will favor strategies that are especially efficient in the preservation of genes, even if that strategy arises from a city of ten thousand virgins serving a single mother. The details of the process are still being worked out, but the resulting rudimentary, functionless ovarian tissue of the workers speaks plainly enough. It can be seen upon dissection and it speaks for, not against, Darwin's theory.

What Harvester Ants Eat

Harvester ants are expected to eat seeds and they do, but they eat much, much more than that. The name "harvester" implies wrongly that the insect is a vegetarian and that it consumes nothing but seeds. Most harvesters are passable hunters and almost all are even better scavengers. When they forage for seeds, they pick them up from the ground or pluck them right off the plant. For example, *Pogonomyrmex subdentatus* of California climbs into the weeds, sinks its teeth into a leaf, and then shakes the plant until ripe seeds drop to the ground (Mallis 1941). The Florida and western harvesters do the same, as do *P. coarctatus* and Mayr's harvester of South America. The booty is carried to the nest and stored in chambers called granaries. Quite a cache is likely to result—two quarts of seeds were discovered in a single nest of the Florida harvester, and 54,000 were counted in the granaries of a western harvester nest (Eddy 1970).

Seeds from over one hundred plant species are on the menu, but some have favored status. Grasses head the list and the best known of these is three-awn: first, because it often grows on the edge of the nest; second, because it has a beard, like the ants that consume it; and third, because of an idea that gave rise to its common name of "ant-rice." Also consumed are love grass, panic grass, crabgrass, centipede grass, buffalo grass, millet, barley, and too many others to mention. Harvesters eat seeds from dozens of plant families beyond the grasses; representatives of these include rattlepod, pine (including pollen), Queen's delight, ragweed, pokeweed, clover, alfalfa, vetch, peppervine, palmetto, buttonweed, nettle, and Mormon tea. An exhaustive list would be hundreds of species long. The ants are not too choosy about seeds, so I have not matched these plants with the particular harvesters that are known to eat them. Plant secretions favored by harvesters include nectar and pine resin (MacKay 1981). Nothing *but* seeds has been reported as food for nine South American and Caribbean species, but this is probably due to severely biased sampling. Field work in South America has been almost nonexistent.

THE LINCECUM HYPOTHESIS

The Lincecum Hypothesis, or the ant-rice story, is a strangely romantic idea from the Civil War era that has now lost favor. This controversy revolved around the claim that harvesters not only collect seeds but also *plant* them and then return to harvest next year's crop. Some writers and researchers wanted to know if this was done intentionally.

It all began with the eccentric physician-naturalist Gideon Lincecum (fig. 3.4) and his observations of the red harvester in central Texas. Lincecum read Darwin's *On the Origin of Species* and followed this with a letter to the father of natural selection, a letter containing additional evidence for the new theory of evolution. This evidence was culled from the natural history of the red harvester ant. He assured the disbelieving evolutionist that seeds are "intentionally planted" (Lincecum 1862).

An expert on European harvesters presented the Lincecum Hypothesis in a general review of harvester ants (Moggridge 1873),

3.4 The grave of Dr. Gideon Lincecum, a former student of the red harvester ant.

but shortly thereafter the great paleontologist Joseph Leidy was the first to dispute openly Lincecum's claim (Remarks on ants 1877). That same year, a Philadelphia minister named H. C. McCook set out for Austin, Texas, where he studied the biology of the red harvester. McCook pitched his tent and dug up many nests, but he was unable to resolve the matter. He agreed that the ants collect and store seeds, even allowing that ant-rice grows on the edge of the nest clearing, but he would not go as far as Lincecum. Maybe the ants were farmers, maybe they weren't (McCook 1882). Darwin's famous colleague in evolution and natural selection, Alfred Russel Wallace, weighed in on the subject in a review of McCook's book for the prestigious journal *Nature* (Wallace 1879). Wallace believed farming possible, but he also viewed the issue as undecided. The members of the Philadelphia Academy of Sciences were less kind; they greeted Lincecum's hypothesis with "a howl of disbelief" (Burkhalter 1965). Wheeler (1910) sided with Darwin, Leidy, and the Academy—he did not believe that the red harvester ant planted seeds intentionally.

It now appears that the ants reject certain seeds from the nest granaries and, since the trash heap is at the edge of the nest, a ring of plants grows and surrounds the nest over time (see fig. 2.3). Seeds are thrown away if they become unsuitable to eat after germination or if they are infected by fungi.

Jerry Lincecum, a descendant of Gideon, gave a talk about Lincecum. He acknowledged the eccentric behavior of his forebear, who must have been a likeable character. Gideon is buried in Austin in the Texas State Cemetery, where he lies only a few feet from Stephen F. Austin. Death had the last laugh on this teller of tall tales. The marker describes him as an internationally known botanist and as a friend of Darwin, and it gives his expiration date as 1873. He was no such botanist, no friend of Darwin (who once said of a Lincecum letter, "Such grammar!"), and the rumor of his death was greatly exaggerated—he was still alive in 1873 and did not die until the following year.

ANTS AS CARNIVORES

Not all ant food is derived from plants. At least some queen harvesters nourish their first brood with an oral secretion derived from fat reserves and wing muscles (Hölldobler 1984). The young of the western harvester eat their little brothers and/or sisters when the queen feeds her first brood with eggs from which larvae could presumably hatch (Nagel and Rettenmeyer 1973). The Florida harvester has a variation on this theme. Its *workers* lay eggs (called trophic eggs) that are eaten by old queens and young larvae (Wilson 1963). No other species is known to do it. This is not infanticide because worker eggs are not viable in any event. Surprisingly, there is not a single case of cannibalism in the familiar sense. Adults do not eat adults of the same species. There is one report of cannibalism in a very broad sense—the rough harvester eats the closely related red one (Hölldobler and Markl 1989).

Most of the harvesters' meat is carved from the exoskeletons of their fellow insects. They would appear to be ideal predators because of their large size, great power, respectable speed, toothy jaws, and—last but not least—potent stinger. Such is not the case. They are said to take little live prey. A prominent exception is the soft white body of the termite. The earliest naturalists saw harvesting of a very different kind when red ants fanned out into the vegetation after spring rains, returning with mouthfuls of swarming termites (fig. 3.5). The Reverend McCook (1879) noted piles of them at a nest entrance, but they were soon taken down into the darkness of subterranean chambers and packed into the meat lockers. The defenseless nature of the termite makes it ideal prey for the red harvester and quite a few others. These "white ants" comprise 66 percent of the rough harvester's insect food (Whitford, Johnson, and Ramirez 1976) and also appear on the menus of the California harvester, the western harvester, the desert harvester *(P. desertorum)*, the Maricopa harvester *(P. maricopa),* and the

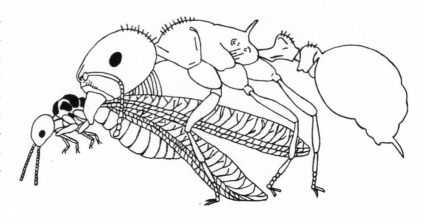

3.5 Harvester ants harvest more than seeds. This worker has captured a termite during the termite's swarming season.

Apache harvester *(P. apache)* (fig. 3.6). Even relatively timid ants take termite prey. These include *Ephebomyrmex imberbiculus* of North America and Mayr's harvester of South America. The huge nuptial swarms of the termite provide a feast the world over. In *The Soul of the White Ant* (Marais 1937), we learn that African swarms are gulped down by everything from ants to apes.

What follows is the first report on the Comanche harvester's diet. I watched them in the heat of several Texas summers among the loblolly pines of Bastrop State Park (fig. 3.7). This fast, gracile species carries a stream of insects and their parts into the nest. Notable were the large numbers of male and queen red imported fire ants that had gone from the extremes of a nuptial flight to the main course of another species' dinner. On days following a rain, the fire ants climb up vegetation and take off into the sky where they mate. Mated queens, or gynes, return to earth soon thereafter, hitting the ground with an audible thump that is surprising for such a small insect. Comanche harvesters brought in dozens of these while I watched; they must take quite a toll over the entire fire ant mating season.

3.6 The Apache harvester. A distinct feature is the deeply notched (light-colored) area, much smaller in all other species, between the base of the antennae and the top of the jaws.

I also saw a large caterpillar struggling

3.7 A Comanche nest among the sandy post oaks of the pine forest in Bastrop State Park, Texas.

against a half dozen or so Comanches, which were carrying it toward their nest. The level of cooperation exhibited that day was not impressive. Up to forty red harvesters have been known to wrestle with such large objects (Wu 1990). Grasshopper legs seem to be enjoyed by ants on both continents. Comanches also relish that most unnatural of grassland foods, the canned tuna fish. Dr. William MacKay tells me that mealworms are accepted in the lab. The Comanche harvester collects seeds of fluffy snake-cotton and many others, including the parakeet seeds I placed nearby as a test of their harvesting abilities.

The carnivorous nature of harvesters has sometimes been questioned, perhaps because of the name itself. Carlos Bruch was an entomologist and an excellent insect photographer who worked in Argentina in the early part of the twentieth century. Bruch (1923) actually witnessed *P. coarctatus* (the biggest harvester of all) carrying a grasshopper leg, saw a cache of insect parts within the nest, and watched the ants as they ate insect pieces that he offered. Nevertheless, Bruch believed that the ants were vegetarians and that his observations must have been spurious in some way. Myrmecologists should be prepared to accept bizarre behavior among their study organisms. The queen of one ant species (not a harvester) feeds only upon the blood of her own offspring, which she obtains by biting them (Peeters 1997).

The Frenchman Pierre Latreille was the first to publish on the harvesters (in 1802), but his denial was of the opposite sort, a denial of the notion that *seeds* are stored. That seemingly defining behavior was perceived by Latreille as a myth. Latreille's knowledge in related matters was enough to save his own life when he was imprisoned during the terror of the French Revolution. He discovered a beetle in his cell and so impressed his visitors with his entomological knowledge that they arranged for his release. The guillotine might have been next. (For further information on the life of Latreille, see Cordier [1833], Dow [1913], or Swainson [1840].)

Other animal foods of the harvesters include carcasses of rattlesnakes, rabbits, rodents, and lizards, living lice from blankets, screwworm maggots pulled from dead and dying animals, ticks, mites, snails, worms, butterflies, millipedes, silverfish, spiders, isopods, cicada nymphs, assassin bugs, bees, beetles, grubs, various larvae, and other ants. Harvesters also eat fungi and animal excretions, such as aphid honeydew, and the feces of just about anything that moves. The western harvester has been seen drinking water from a shell, and the desert harvester accepted pure water in a lab trial. The rough harvester accepts water according to some, but rejects it according to others. I have seen the red harvester drinking from rain pools, surrounding the miniature water holes like herds of tiny cows.

FEEDING BEHAVIORS

Surprisingly little is known about feeding behavior because it goes on inside the nest. There have been a few laboratory observations on the red harvester, the western, and a lesser known species, *E. imberbiculus*. The literature is sometimes contradictory. Feeding does not involve regurgitation between adults, although this is routine for many ants that carry food in a crop, or "communal stomach" (Wheeler 1902a). The youngest larvae do receive food from the adults by regurgitation (Wheeler 1928). They eat while lying on their soft, white backs (larva illustrated in the drawing of *P. barbatus*). Older larvae use special hairs on their bellies that hold solid food in place while their mandibles gnaw away at insects and seeds (Petralia and Vinson 1979).

Surprisingly, considering the most famous attribute of the harvesters, few comments exist in the literature on seed preparation. The Florida harvester husks its seeds before storing them (Hutchins 1958), a task that might be the specialty of a specific worker subclass (Oster and Wilson 1978). These millers are said to be giant, huge-headed bruisers, which seldom if ever forage. Another hypothesis has the large workers acting as nurses to the brood (Gordon 1984b). The western (Dean 1905) and the red harvester (Lincecum 1862) also husk their seeds before storage, but neither the South American *P. coarctatus* (Hubrich 1929) nor the tiny North American *Ephebomyrmex imberbiculus* (Wheeler 1902a) does so. The tough outer coating is not removed until time to eat, when the workers split the good parts with their tiny siblings, the larvae. One of the South American Andean species chews grass seeds into a paste before eating them (Goetsch 1935).

Observations of food-handling differences among various species is interesting in light of the evolutionary tree that I have reconstructed for the harvesters. According to those results, one could say that *Ephebomyrmex* and South American *Pogonomyrmex* are generally more primitive than North American *Pogonomyrmex*. It is consistent with this generalization that the most derived ("advanced") forms of food processing are seen among the North American *Pogonomyrmex*.

Not all of the stored seeds are destined for consumption. A seed that begins to grow (germinate) is sometimes thrown on the trash heap, as are seeds with a fungus infection. The red harvester is not so finicky. It eats seeds whether they are germinating or not (Wu 1990). The rough harvester prefers uninfected seeds (Knoch, Faeth, and Arnott 1993). The western harvester is finicky about being finicky—it avoided moldy seeds according to one report (Crist and Friese 1993) but accepted them according to another (Knoch, Faeth, and Arnott 1993). Germination can be prevented or minimized if seeds that become soaked by rain in the nest are taken outside and dried in the sun. Several harvester species are known to do this. In cold climates at least, seeds are not eaten while the sluggish ants overwinter in the dormant stage (MacKay and MacKay 1984).

The Huntress at Work

Harvester ants forage for food in two ways. Individual foraging is the most primitive and by far the most common hunting strategy. Individual foragers leave the nest on their own, do not follow trails, and therefore are not seen traveling in long columns. Only a few exclusively individual foragers are likely to be encountered by general collectors or by accident. The Maricopa harvester is foremost among these.

Group foraging evolved more recently, is used by only a few species, and is confined to North America with one possible exception (Goetsch 1934). Group foragers include the red harvester, the rough harvester, the Florida harvester, *P. salinus,* and the western harvester, which apparently reverts to individual hunting on occasion (Fewell 1988). The most common North American harvesters are these group foragers, and that behavior is one of the reasons for their success. Hundreds of their workers can be seen marching in long red columns on trails up to 2 inches wide and 100 feet or more in length. The California harvester is also an occasional group forager (Whitford 1976).

There is a third component to hunting behavior that occurs among the group foragers and among some of the individual foragers as well. This is called recruitment (Hölldobler and Wilson 1970). Because droves of huntresses can be called forth to a pile of seeds or insects, it is tempting to describe the result as group foraging, but it is not. Recruitment occurs along a chemical trail laid down by the ant that made the initial discovery. It is sometimes reinforced by those who follow, sometimes not.

All harvesters forage during the day, but some also hunt at night. No nocturnal hunting has been reported for the Florida harvester (Golley and Gentry 1964) and a few fairly common species, including the Comanche ant. These two species always close their nests at night, and that easily accounts for their stay-at-home behavior.

Searching for food by temperate species is a seasonal activity that begins in the spring and ends in the fall when nests close up for the overwintering phase. During this phase the ants are dormant but not in a true state of hibernation. Useful generalizations have exceptions and *P. subdentatus* of California is one of them; it forages on cold November days (Mallis 1941). Tropical species presumably forage year-round. Within the active season there are days of intense activity, and there is a time of day in desert summer when activity ceases due to the unbearable heat of the soil. This begins around noon and lasts until the middle or late afternoon. There is a soil temperature range for optimal hunting, which is typically 68–122°F (Lavigne 1969), and the western harvester checks this by running around in circles just outside the nest. When the ground has warmed up from the chill of night, foraging begins. Intense activity occurs on days following a rain when the ground is cooler and insect prey is about. Each foraging ant makes several forays per day at speeds of about 0.1 miles per hour, increasing when making a successful return with booty. Large nests of the rough harvester look like frenzied Lilliputian cities as foragers stream in at a rate of 116 per minute for a total of maybe fifty thousand trips per day with a task force of 1,500 ants (Whitford and Ettershank 1975). They typically carry loads comparable to their own weight of about nine milligrams (50,000 ants per pound).

Navigation depends upon sight (e.g., bushes near the nest) and the direction of polarized sunlight, but chemical trails are sometimes laid down when a foraging windfall is encountered. This depends upon the species. An active forager can be slow, steady, and unspectacular (e.g., the red harvester) or comical in its gait and carriage (the Comanche harvester). Comanches run erratically with stops and starts as they tuck their rear end beneath the rest of the body, looking like tiny dogs with tails between their legs. This tucking behavior might be used to lay down chemicals. The Apache, desert, and California harvesters *raise* the rear end, presumably to keep it away from the searing heat of the soil (Wheeler 1902a,b). This might be in addition to a lowering behavior like that of the Comanche ant.

Journeys into the hostile surroundings of the nest can be as far as 160 feet (Gentry and Stiritz 1972). This is roughly equivalent to a 10-mile trip for a human. Imagine walking this far to the supermarket and returning with dinner only 60 percent of the time. This is the experience of the desert harvester—ants often return with nothing in their jaws (Davidson 1977).

The most interesting things happen when food is finally discovered. If the victim is a manageable living insect it will be attacked, killed, and cut up into little pieces (Eddy 1970). The western harvester is a true Darwinian in its tactics, pursuing wounded bugs with greater zeal than healthy ones. When *P. vermiculatus* of the Andes finds food, it signals this to its nestmates by wiggling its abdomen and opening its jaws (Goetsch 1934). Large prey, such as caterpillars, must be dealt with in force by up to forty Amazons. Sometimes their sisters dig the soil out from under the burden, perhaps making it easier to move.

The Maricopa harvester is impatient of chemical recruitment—its recruits are carried passively to the site in the jaws of those who know the way. Some harvesters carry each other in a stereotyped way by clamping the jaws around the waist. This is thought to be more advanced, or at least more modern, than the other method in which ants grab their nestmates any old way (Möglich and Hölldobler 1974).

There are some strange adaptations that presumably increase the efficiency of the hunt. If a Florida harvester happens upon a hole with a sweet liquid inside that is too low to reach, it drops pebbles into the hole until the liquid level rises high enough to drink (Morrill 1972). Mayr's harvester does something similar when it drops pebbles into sweet puddles (Kugler and Hincapie 1983). When the pebbles are coated with the syrup they are carried back to the nest. This might be more efficient than drinking. Since adult harvesters do not share food through regurgitation, a well-filled crop would be of no use to adult nestmates.

The western harvester has specializations too, but of a different kind. Foragers tend to be faithful to both particular trails and particular seed types. They have been seen licking honeydew directly off the bodies of aphids (plant lice) (Jones 1929), but here we also see a *lack* of specialization. Many ants treat aphids like little cows, taking honeydew while guarding them from predators and protecting them at night by moving them into the nest until morning. There is no record of this behavior among harvesters. (By the way, honeydew isn't as sweet as it sounds, although it contains plenty of sugar. This nectar comes from the aphid's rear end.) Most harvesters do have a specialization in the form of a beard, which is used to carry soil, but they never carry food in these baskets, at least not in the wild. However, it has been seen in the lab (Spangler and Rettenmeyer 1966).

Some plants are killed in the seed stage when harvesters collect and eat them. The situation is very different for the California poppy bush, which actually benefits when its seeds are trundled off. *Pogonomyrmex subnitidus* collects its seeds but rejects them at the nest after removing and eating a tasty seed appendage called an elaiosome (Bullock 1974). By that time the seed has traveled quite a distance, reducing the problems of competition with its parent plant and other poppy bushes. In other words, it has been dispersed by the ant. The California harvester does the same thing for poisonous jimson weed (Snelling and George 1979).

Harvesters are dedicated huntresses. One of the first publications on the subject reported a beetle that flew off from a nest with several red harvesters still attached by their jaws (Buckley 1860). They will enter bees' nests to get pollen (Bohart and Knowlton 1953), and when holed up in the nest by summer's heat, they will dart out in the cooling shadow of a passing human.

Chapter 4
Defending the Nest

*The great red monster begins in earnest to crush and
slay every one that comes in range of his death-dealing jaws.*

—GIDEON LINCECUM,
SPEAKING OF THE RED HARVESTER ANT

Enemies of Harvester Ants

The enemies of the western harvester include predators, parasitoids, parasites, and competitors. There is at least one enemy from each of the first three categories that specializes on harvesters; the fourth category includes humans. Almost nothing is known about the enemies of the South American ants, and general ignorance about the biologies on that continent is the single biggest hole in the study of the harvesters.

The most famous natural enemy is a dragonlike lizard of North American deserts known as the horned toad, horny toad, horned frog, or horned lizard of the genus *Phrynosoma* (fig. 4.1) (Whiting, Dixon, and Murray 1993). They are closely related to the common iguanas. Horned toads favor harvesters, and when the ants disappear from an area due to habitat change or the encroachment of fire ants, the lizards disappear too. About half a dozen species have been reported to eat harvesters. A single reptile can inflict serious damage on a colony as it laps up passing victims from its perch on or near the mound. Red harvester colonies have been extinguished in this way; an actual count of victims was made

4.1 *The horned lizard is an enemy of the harvester ant. This lizard is exaggerated for effect, being only several inches long in reality. (Lizard modified from a U.S. Fish and Wildlife Service photograph taken by W. Byron Miller.)*

at a desert harvester mound where 111 sisters were eaten, a large fraction of the population (Whitford and Bryant 1979).

The ants defend themselves with a swarming attack called "mobbing," which sometimes drives away the monster. A lizard besieged but determined to stay will remain motionless as dozens of ants crawl over its scaly armor, biting and stinging as they go. The "toads" have an immunity or defense against ant venom in the form of a detoxifying substance in their blood plasma (Schmidt, Sherbrooke, and Schmidt 1989), and when mobbed they simply hunker down with closed eyes until the ants leave. By the turn of the century there was a thriving horny toad trade in which Easterners were supplied with pets from the desert southwest. In 1915 one writer still counted thirty "toads" per acre even though the export business had been a healthy concern for years (Winton 1915). Horned lizards are scarce now and protected by law.

The red harvester has more predators than any other species

of harvester, according to the vast literature on the subject. Birds are prominent on the predator list, including chickens, mocking-birds, grackles, plovers, owls, nighthawks, flycatchers, cardinals, shrikes, blue jays, woodpeckers, and doves (Mitchell and Pierce 1912). Newly mated queens are large, fat, and juicy and are there-fore special favorites of the feathered horde; blue jays once ate an entire mating swarm (the population of mating males and females, which can number in the hundreds or thousands). Tree frogs and spadefoot toads enjoy them too.

The western harvester is plagued by a similar host of backboned demons: sand lizards, fence lizards, various toads, sparrows, grouse, wrens, flickers, and starlings. The rough harvester has a stealthier foe in the form of the plains blind snake (Schmidt and Schmidt 1989). It is a strange creature on several counts. Small and worm-like, it has tiny rudimentary eyes beneath see-through scales. It can smell the chemicals of the ant trail, and when it traces this to a nest it rubs on its own version of insect repellent—a mixture of feces and gland secretions that ants understandably steer clear of. The snake burrows into the mound and devours its prey.

Collared lizards and fence lizards feed upon *Pogonomyrmex salinus,* as do blackbirds, meadowlarks, sparrows, and thrashers (Knowlton 1974). Oddly enough, the widely distributed and greatly studied Florida harvester has no known vertebrate predators. This is doubly strange because it was the first pogo known to science (described by Latreille in 1802), and it has received a great deal of attention in the literature. In South America the only predation records are of lizards. A gecko eats Mayr's harvester and there is a single lizard that eats two of the lesser known ants.

There are invertebrate predators and enemies too. Ants, in-cluding other harvesters and even their own species, are among the worst offenders. Some of these troublemakers build their nests on the mounds or clearings of the harvesters and harry the har-vesters as they go about their work. Some steal booty from return-ing foragers. One competing species actually drops pebbles into harvester nest entrances, thereby getting a head start on hunting for food while the temporarily trapped creatures dig their way out (Gordon 1988).

Others, including army ants, seize and eat harvesters. Army ants, although blind, are formidable enemies (fig. 4.2). After one

4.2 *A blind legionary or army ant* (Labidus coecus), *which preys upon harvesters.*

such battle with army ants, all the harvesters that were still walking had two heads. One was their own, the other a severed one
from the body of an army ant. The trash heap was stacked with
legionary corpses (Wheeler 1910). I have witnessed colonies of the
red harvester and the Comanche go at it with imported fire ants.
These were real donnybrooks and it was almost comical to see the
much larger harvesters hiding in the grass tops. Nevertheless, their
nests were still there when I checked days later. Once, challenged
by a much smaller, black species, each huge harvester was observed
to kill a dozen or more of the enemy before moving on to the next
engagement (Reading of letter 1866).

The rough harvester raids colonies of both the red and desert
species and removes the brood, eating some and perhaps raising
others to become working members of their own colony (Hölldobler and Markl 1989). Killing its own kind has an interesting
effect on the California harvester—the killers return to their own
nest and linger inside (Devita 1979).

Black widows and other spiders make webs at the edge of the
nest and snare the Florida harvester, the red, the rough, the California, the Comanche, the montane, the western, and two lesser
known North American ants (McCook 1879; MacKay 1982a;
Gentry 1974). I captured a small spider of some kind in its web as
it fed upon the Comanche harvester, but this first record of a

Comanche predator remains on my shelf in alcohol, awaiting proper identification. The web was high up in grass that surrounded the nest clearing.

An exhaustive list of harvester predators would have to include robber flies, wasps, assassin bugs, ant-lions, beetles, sun spiders (weird, voracious arachnids), and dragonflies. Assassin bugs act like tiny horned lizards as they lurk along foraging trails, but they drive their beaks into passing victims after capturing them with raptorial forelegs (Cade, Simpson, and Breland 1978).

The strangest parasite of harvesters is a worm called *Skrjabinoptera phrynosoma* (Lee 1955, 1957). This nematode is a reptile specialist that attacks both the harvester and the harvester's worst natural enemy. It gets into the stomach of the horned lizard by getting into the harvester when the ant is still a wormlike juvenile in the nest. The death of the mother worm is required for this because her dried, dead body must be scavenged by a worker ant, taken back to the nest, and fed to the young ant. The worm's eggs are still inside her when she is eaten. Young worms hatch inside the ant and remain there until the larval ant metamorphoses, goes outside, and is snapped up by a passing horned toad. When the infected ant is eaten by this lizard, the life cycle of the worm is completed as female worms with their eggs are excreted with the feces of the lizard. Considering the likelihood of success at each step of this tortuous path, it appears that the worms must produce huge numbers of eggs, which is normal for parasites.

Two harvester ant species are parasites of other harvester ants. *Pogonomyrmex anergismus* (Johnson 1995) and *P. colei* (Rissing 1983) live in the nests of both the red and the rough and in the nests of the rough only (respectively). Common names for these two would be "the workerless harvester" and "Cole's harvester." These ants have sexuals—males and reproductive females—but no workers. They are fed by the host ants whose nests they invade. Such social parasites, or inquilines, are rarely encountered.

More common parasites include fungi and at least some of the mites that are found on larvae and adults. I have seen mites on several South American species that are known from only a few individuals, so these external parasites must be fairly common. An Argentine biologist observed some *P. coarctatus* sunning themselves outside the nest while tiny pseudoscorpions clung to their bodies (Hubrich 1929). (Sunning activity has been seen in North

America too. On warm days following cold spells, red harvesters will gather or "snuggle" outside the nest in fist-sized clumps [Mc-Cook 1879].) There have been no reports of pseudoscorpions on North American ants in all two hundred years of literature. Sometimes these tiny arachnids are merely "accidental tourists" hitching a ride, but others do indeed kill and devour leaf-cutter ants. It is unknown which is the case for those clinging to the harvesters.

A parasitoid is a creature that is parasitic in one phase of life but not in another. The worm described above is a true parasite because it is never free-living. The only known parasitoids of North American harvesters are some flies and closely related wasps that specialize variously on the red, western, rough, and Maricopa species. The parasitoid sphecid wasp is quite bold, actually entering the mound to extract its prey, which will be stung, paralyzed, and whisked aloft in the weirdest way—stuffed into a special clamp at the end of the abdomen (Evans 1962; Evans and West-Eberhard 1970). This clamp carries the victim back to the wasp nest where an egg is laid upon the paralyzed unfortunate (fig. 4.3). The ant will be eaten alive by the wasp larva when it hatches. The sight of a wasp carrying an ant in this way is startling because one expects it to be carried in the jaws or with the legs—at least near the *front*

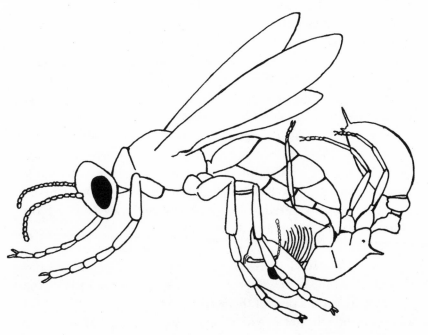

4.3 *This* Clypeadon *wasp is harvesting a harvester. It hunts this single species and nothing else as food for its larvae. (Modified from Evans and West-Eberhard 1970.)*

end. As many as fifty paralyzed ants can be found in piles in a single wasp nest.

Equally odd is another wasp that apparently attacks *E. cunicularius* of South America (Gemignani 1933). It's not clear if it is a specialist on harvesters or not. This wasp's unlikely life cycle starts out as an egg on a plant. A tiny, flattened larva called a planidium hatches from the egg, grabs a passing worker ant, and is carried into the depths of the nest where it attaches to an ant larva. When the ant larva becomes a pupa the parasitoid will begin eating it. This is similar to the worm life cycle, but there is no second host (e.g., a lizard) in this case.

Enemies that compete with harvesters for limited space and food are humans (urban development), rodents (which leave gaping holes when they raid the seed granaries of large mounds), and other ants. Some of these competing ants are fellow harvesters, including the trio of desert, rough, and California, and the duo of the red and the rough. Competition within the species has been observed for several of these as well. The Maricopa harvester drags other Maricopas (trespassing from other nests) as much as 50 feet from the nest before releasing them.

Young harvester colonies tend to be more ready to fight than old ones (Gordon 1991). One of the most striking examples of fighting within the species is that of newly mated queens, which battle over burrows that will become incipient nests. The female that started excavations is usually the winner. When virgin queens of *P. coarctatus* were raised from pupae in test tubes, they mutilated and killed one another (Hubrich 1929). It's not clear if this is territoriality among sisters or if the females were from distantly related nests to begin with.

The preceding list of enemies seems impressive, but considering the large numbers and high profile of harvesters (literally in the case of their mounds), these prominent targets seem to suffer from very few attacks. I have never seen birds on the huge nests, pecking at streams of red ants as if *they* were the seeds. Nor have I seen them moving up and down the trails, picking off foragers. The relative immunity of these ants in the wild is striking.

A South American natural enemy of the red imported fire ant, a scuttle fly of the family Phoridae, was about to be released in the United States at the time of this writing (Kleiner 1997). The larval fly feeds inside the ant's head, which eventually falls off. It will be interesting to see if this fly will also attack native species like the harvester ants. We are told it will not.

Houseguests

Harvester nests can hold twelve thousand or more ants in accommodations that must rival the Pentagon in relative size, but the deep, numerous, and dark chambers of the ant city house friend and foe alike. Some denizens of the nest are beneficial, some harmful, and the status of others is unknown. Three such symbionts seem to be more common than others: beetles, silverfish, and other ants.

Beetles can be found among heaps of insect fragments and seeds in the storage chambers (Hubrich 1929), while silverfish scuttle about elusively and tiny thief ants presumably make off with stored food (Hutchins 1967). These close relatives of the fire ant actually build their nests inside the harvester mound. The Florida harvester shares its home with a rare sand cockroach and with millipedes, silverfish, beetles, mites, and springtails that live in the seed granaries (Porter 1985). The springtails fall prey to a spider that specializes on them. When the harvesters emigrate to a new home the killer spider goes with them.

Mites cling to the head, legs, and abdomen of harvester ants. Some are true parasites of the ants, but others are scavengers, fungus-eaters, or hitchhikers. The western harvester also has beetles, silverfish, and springtails but its zoo is a little different. Termites, ants, and "ground pearls"—bugs that are used to make varnish in tropical countries—live there too (Wheeler and Wheeler 1986). The strangest guest is the horseshoe crab beetle (Moody and Foster 1979). It is half the size of an ant or even smaller, and it rides around on the ants' backs (fig. 4.4). The harvesters seem to co-exist peacefully with it even though the beetle feeds on secretions of the ants. Strong armor and other defenses suggest that its ancestors were less welcome.

The menagerie of the rough harvester boasts of a tiny cricket that licks its food from its hosts (Wheeler and Wheeler 1986). Beetles and silverfish are expected, but the list also includes fly larvae, moth larvae, termites, cicada nymphs, bugs, and the Jerusalem cricket or "child of the earth." The nest is also visited by something not reported for other harvesters—the pronghorn antelope. These large mammals browse outside on Texas filaree, a favored

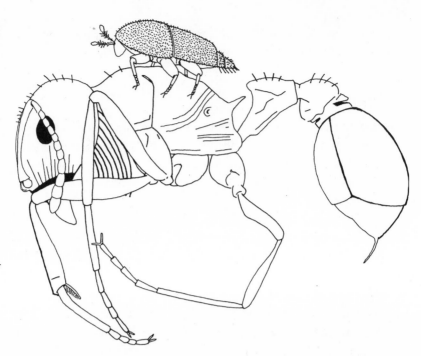

grass that grows around the edge of the rough harvester's nest (Whitford, Forbes, and Kerley 1995).

A kind of scarab beetle is common in the nests of quite a few harvesters (Cazier and Mortenson 1965). The ants have mixed reactions to it. Sometimes it is dragged out of the nest, sometimes it is dragged into it. The ants don't eat the beetle, at least not entirely. The beetle specialists tell us that ants treat them like dairy cows; they lick secretions from glands in the beetles' shoulder area. However, one review of the subject not only questioned this but also reported the beetle as a predator of ant larvae within the nest. It is not always clear what is going on with the harvester ants and these guests.

The red harvester is visited by beetles, silverfish, the little cricket, and flies. One unpublished study reported that houseguests of this ant are uncommon in east-central Texas. An extensive search of nests in the College Station area turned up the cricket and nothing else (Mangrum 1954).

Three South American ants are known to have houseguests. Marcus's harvester and *E. cunicularius* have beetles, whereas the odorous harvester *(E. odoratus)* dwells under a rock with a close relative of the fire ants (Kusnezov 1949).

The fluffy chaff piles of the Apache garbage heap are infested with termites (Wheeler 1902b). Other North American harvesters have symbionts but there is nothing significantly different about those guests. Such ants with common names are the Apache, California, desert, montane, owyhee, and Maricopa harvester. Those without common names are *P. magnacanthus*, *P. subdentatus*, and *P. subnitidus*.

Attack and Defense

Some harvester ants defend their nests vigorously, while others run and hide. In 1884, a writer with firsthand experience called the red harvester "the worst ant in Texas" (Nehrling 1884). Turkeys can be paralyzed and pigs killed by the stings. When they sting humans the result is always painful and sometimes life threatening. This has earned for many North American species a spot on the list of medically important arthropods (Pittaway 1991). That list contains large common ones like the Florida harvester and the red harvester, but most of the other big ones should be there too. Several people have died in Texas and Oklahoma, and there must have been many more deaths over the years and in quite a few other states (Young and Howell 1964).

The ant uses both ends of its body in an attack, but the jaws are used merely to obtain a purchase, to anchor the front end so that the stinger can be driven into the flesh. What can happen next is a litany of discomforts: sensation of ripping muscles and tendons, vomiting, swelling, twenty-four-hour ache, pain in armpits and muscles, oozing lymph fluid, anaphylactic shock, itching, labored breath, angiodema (swollen vessels), wheezing, laryngeal edema, hives, nausea, intense pain for one to four hours, "thrilling" sensation, burning, sweating, welts, soreness for up to four days, ruptured red blood cells, piloerection (hair standing on end), faintness, and dizziness. Note that the list includes anaphylactic shock (Pinnas et al. 1977), an extreme sensitivity to injection of foreign bodies into one's system, which can result in death, sometimes resulting from respiratory failure (strangled breathing pipes from swollen tissue). A fear of impending death is commonly reported by victims. One odd side effect is an irritability that others will interpret as bad temper. I, and therefore my companions, experienced this when I was stung on the thigh by *Pogonomyrmex subnitidus* in the California mountains. (This summary has been prepared from the entire literature and a given individual is not likely to experience all of the effects listed above.)

Recommended treatment in general is a thorough washing of the wound area with soap and water followed by an ice pack (Goddard 1993). Those with an allergy to ant venom might need the epinephrine and/or antihistamines that are available in portable injection kits. A very old publication (Hunter 1912) advocates ammonia taken internally—a treatment no longer recommended. An even older treatment for ant sting is that of Pliny, an ancient Roman, who prescribed the heart of a bat. This remedy can be rejected with complete confidence. There is no report of disease transmission by the sting of the harvester ant. See Rodgers and Matyunas (1994) for an overview of treatment for stings from ants.

The amount of venom injected in each sting is minute, about 20 micrograms. It would require the stings of 50,000,000 ants to fill up a 1-liter bottle. One measure of the danger of the sting is in something called the LD_{50} dose for mice, a dose that is lethal for about half of the animals that receive it, which can be as low as 0.125 mg/kg (for the Maricopa harvester—the dose is higher for other harvesters) (Schmidt 1990). This means that, if one-eighth of a milligram of venom were given to each rodent in a group of one-kilogram rodents (big but hypothetical rodents), about half of all the subjects stung would die. In reality the mouse would be much smaller, but so would the dose required to kill it.

The sting of Mayr's harvester of South America isn't as bad. The ant can't be forced to sting a human, although several South American species can. These include the mighty *P. coarctatus,* the slightly less mighty Marcus's harvester, and the gracile *E. cunicularius* and *E. brevibarbis* (Kusnezov 1954). The Florida harvester *(P. badius)* was the first one discovered; one might assume incorrectly that the species name refers to the painful sting or to a "bad" temper. It doesn't. It merely refers to the rusty brown color of the ant.

If you're wondering if queens sting, the answer is yes. (Males can't—the stinger is a modified egg-laying device or ovipositor, which the males lack.) The stinger often breaks off in the wound because of a series of sharp barbs at its tip. This is called autotomy and is a form of insurance against removal made famous by the honeybee. In both insects, the muscles around the stinger keep pumping venom even after the eviscerated body has been brushed from the skin.

The harvester has a panoply of weapons in addition to its famous "business end" (fig. 4.5). One offensive weapon is a pair of jaws that is needed for the stinging response, but which can be used alone against insect enemies. In fact, the venom might be useless against many arthropod foes because it seems to have evolved as a defense against mammals like us (Schmidt and Blum 1978a,b). A caterpillar stung eleven times was hardly affected even though a much larger mouse might be killed with only a few jabs. How did this come about? It centers on the seed-harvesting habit itself. The harvester stores seeds in granaries in highly visible nests, which are sought out by seed-loving rodents in the desert. Gaping holes in the mounds can be left by kangaroo rats, which burrow right through the gravel (Clark and Comanor 1973). The tiny jaws of a harvester could dismember a caterpillar in a hurry but it would take something systemic to stop such a huge, furry invader. An injection of venom through a hypodermic needle and into the bloodstream does nicely.

The remaining weapons are more purely defensive in nature, and a complete armor-plating of tough exoskeleton is foremost among them. The adult exoskeleton is hardened by proteins and a modified sugar called "chitin" that can be difficult to penetrate in

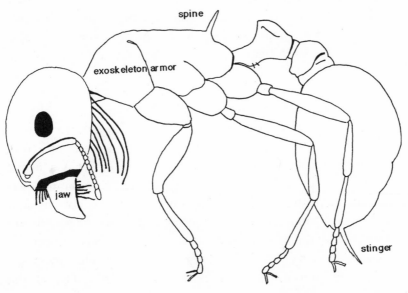

4.5 The armament of the red harvester consists of jaws, a tough exoskeleton, a pair of spines, and painful venom delivered by the sting, or stinger.

a fight. This was tested many years ago by William Morton Wheeler (1900) who placed a "jumping ant" with snapping jaws into an arena. Several other ant species were forced to face the ant. A red harvester, an army ant, and some tough, primitive types were among the victims. Wheeler found that the jumping ant had the most difficulty with the harvester and he attributed this relative invulnerability to a tougher suit of armor. Many harvesters have a pair of upwardly projecting spines on their back, which defend the narrow waist region, certainly the weakest part of the body (see fig. 4.5). Fighting ants grip one another in this area and it is common to see ants that have been cut in half through the waist.

The last article of the built-in panoply is a controversial one. Quite a few harvesters have small lobes or projections jutting out from the face just below the attachment of the antennae or "feelers" to the head. The myrmecologist who described P. lobatus thought that these toothlike structures protected the feelers (Santschi 1921). An enemy in a head-on brawl would have difficulty getting close to the antennae with those bulges in the way. My study of the evolution of the harvesters suggests that this has evolved on many occasions, but some of the species that bear them are those that *retreat* from a fight, and some brawling types lack them altogether. Maybe the "cheek pieces" of the harvester helmet have a different function, if they have a function at all.

The remaining defenses are behavioral, and one of these involves tool use. The word "tool" is used here in its broadest sense because the ant doesn't make the object, it merely picks up something close at hand and drops it on the head of something else. Sometimes the harvester drops the tool into the nest entrance of a nearby competitor, sealing the enemy inside while the harvester gets a head start on foraging. It has been known to land on the ant-lion at the bottom of its lethal pit (Wu 1990).

Closing and moving the nest are often used as defenses against enemies (see chapter 2). Some ants move just the nest entrance from time to time. The California harvester does this. It has a strong offense too, being described as the worst ant of the Sonoran Desert (Wheeler and Wheeler 1973). This ant keeps its trash out of sight by burying it underground, which might make it harder for an enemy to find the nest. Foragers also sometimes remain inside if a predator is lurking nearby. This keeps the colony profile low.

A South American harvester keeps a defensive vigil by posting at least one sentinel at the door (Goetsch 1932). It is common for harvesters to carry their young into the depths of the nest when it is broken open. Several North American species have a special task force of defenders that keep an eye on things, and all of the large, common species send out their defensive legions when the sexuals leave the nest for the mating swarm. Like a sea of tiny robots the workers mill about in an ever widening circle, clearing the ground of anything that might threaten the emerging queens and males. Human observers have a knee-jerk tendency to backpedal slowly as the ranks of this guard swell in number.

The strangest behaviors of all are those displayed by several North American ants: they rear up on their hind legs, waggle their back ends, and point their jaws at the intruder (Cole 1968). Sometimes the insect freezes and waves its antennae. I don't know what good this does. More understandable docility is the retreat to cover shown by most of the small harvesters. They crawl under rocks or hide in the nest. Danger is signaled to the colony by chemicals and sounds or vibrations, the subjects of the next section on communication.

Chapter 5

Communication, Sex, and Anatomy

The groan of ants who undertake
Gigantic loads for honour's sake,
(Their sinews creak, their breath comes thin)
— ROBERT GRAVES,
LOST LOVE

Communication, Chemistry, Sound, and Death by Injection

Harvester ants have internal glands arranged from head to stinger. Six glands are mentioned in the literature with the names mandibular, postpharyngeal, sternal, Dufour's, convoluted, and poison (Baroni Urbani 1993). The contents of the metapleural gland are not mentioned in harvester literature, and this is odd since its presence is near diagnostic for the ant clan. The metapleural gland generally seems to have antibiotic activity (Hölldobler and Wilson 1990).

Work on harvester chemistry and sound began with two students of W. M. Wheeler. Axel Melander and C. T. Brues (1906) were the first to perform a chemical assay on the body fluids of harvesters, using the red variety. They found no formic acid in the venom. This is interesting because there is a tendency to link all ants with formic acid. After all, they do comprise the family Formicidae. A modern ant chemist once tasted venom and described the sensation as "corrosive" (Schmidt 1989). A myrmecologist collected various harvesters, removed their stingers, and found no distinctive flavor (Hunt 1973).

Both Henry McCook and Gideon Lincecum had something to say about the odor of the ants. Lincecum (1866) sniffed the red harvester and smelled nothing. He dutifully noted the absence of formic acid. McCook (1879) was on the trail of something else. He realized that the ants leave an odor on objects that attracts their nestmates. We now call this a recruitment or trail pheromone. The molecular gauntlet thrown down by Melander and Brues was picked up by E. O. Wilson and others in midcentury when they investigated the necrophoric response (the carrying of the dead). When a harvester dies there is something about it that causes its sisters to carry the corpse to the garbage pile. Recently expired sisters aren't eaten or buried. They're just thrown away. The stimulus was found to be of a chemical nature—the esters and fatty acids of a decomposing body (Wilson, Durlach, and Roth 1958).

The most talked about communication chemical is the alarm pheromone that is found in the mandibular gland of the head. It is a hydrocarbon with the imposing name of 4-methyl-3-heptanone. This was unknown from any natural source until it was found in a harvester ant (McGurk et al. 1966). Edward O. Wilson knew something was there, as its odor was detectable almost two feet away, but he didn't know what the substance was. The head apparently contained 6.3×10^{16} molecules of unknown identity (Wilson and Bossert 1963).

The pheromone's effects depend upon the concentration present. At low concentrations it excites the ants and makes them run around in circles. At high concentrations they begin digging. How might this last response have come about during the process of evolution? A collapsed mound would certainly be cause for alarm and there would be many ants secreting the chemical. Experiments have shown that harvesters prefer their natural alarm pheromone when given a choice from similar molecules (Blum, Doolittle, and Beroza 1971). The ants can even detect the chirality of the molecule (the arrangement of the atoms), and they prefer one chiral form of 4-methyl-3-heptanone over the other (Benthuysen and Blum 1974). Most of the common North American species have been tested and all of these have this same chemical. It serves at least two purposes beyond alarm: it summons the crowd to the mating rituals and it repels fire ants.

The chemical ants use to lead their nestmates to food is the recruitment pheromone. It is stored in the poison gland but there is no mention of the molecule(s) responsible. In at least some species recruitment pheromone is secreted when foragers attack difficult prey, such as large insects. One report says that the western harvester does not use the trail pheromone under natural conditions (Melvin 1968). Other ants besides harvesters have a trail pheromone that is similar to the harvester's. The Florida harvester will follow some of their trails (Attygalle and Morgan 1985).

Of all the potions in the harvester arsenal, its venom is of greatest interest to humans because of its painful and sometimes deadly effects. These ants have the most toxic insect venoms known (Schmidt 1986), and the richest source of enzymes ever reported from arthropods was the venom of the Florida harvester (Schmidt and Blum 1978c). This was also the first report of a venom with lipase activity. (A lipase is an enzyme that breaks apart a molecule called a lipid. Lipids include the fats stored in human adipose cells, which are also broken down by the esterase of the Florida harvester's venom.) There are also hemolytic agents (which rupture blood cells), neurotoxins, hyaluronidase (a chemical that breaks up tissues and allows the venom to spread), phospholipase (breaks down fatty molecules like those in our cell membranes), histamine (causes inflammation and swelling of the wound area), phosphatase (a cause of allergic response), various proteins, kinins (cause pain), and amino acids. Amino acids comprise proteins and the unique peptide of the red harvester, which is called "barbatolysin" (Bernheimer, Avigad, and Schmidt 1980). Barbatolysin ruptures red blood cells, making this ant venom the most hemolytic of all. Blood clotting is also impaired by the presence of an anticoagulant. The Maricopa harvester has kinin in its venom and Wheeler's harvester has something like it (Piek et al. 1989). Both substances cause pain. According to one report, venom is actually synthesized in the convoluted gland and stored in the poison gland (Baroni Urbani 1993).

Other chemicals have been isolated or at least indicated by their effects. The homing signal is a molecule or mixture of molecules that marks the vicinity of the nest so that foragers can find their way home. Dufour's gland dispenses it. The complex mixture contains a variety of hydrocarbons (up to thirty or more) and a sesquiterpenoid (a type of hydrocarbon-containing molecule) that might also be used in communication (Billen et al. 1987). Larvae are recognized and fed on the basis of their odor (Wilson 1971), and it is an odor that attracts a spider to harvester ant prey (Hölldobler 1970). Workers prefer not only the smell of their own alarm pheromones but the smell of their own nest materials over that of other colonies as well. Students in our undergraduate lab at the University of Texas verified this statistically by measuring the amount of time an ant spends on its own soil versus the time it spends on other soils. She spends more time on her own nest soil.

Regarding other chemicals, one report states that the exoskeleton of the red harvester inhibits the viability of *Narcissus* pollen (Hull and Beattie 1988). The metapleural gland, mentioned earlier, secretes an antibiotic in some ants. Extracts of the rough harvester contain the possible antibiotic phenyl acetic acid (Fales et al. 1992). However, secretions of the Florida harvester do not defend them against fungi (Wilson 1971). No chemical has been isolated from the South American species, but Marcus's harvester does have acids and bases in its venom apparatus (Marcus 1953). Chemical analysis reveals little resemblance between *P. salinus* and its visually apparent mimic *Messor lobognathus* (do Nascimento et al. 1993). It has been thought that *Messor* (also an ant) benefits from a resemblance to the harvester, which bears a more potent sting.

Axel Melander (1902) was the first to report stridulation, a behavior that produces sounds that humans can hear but ants can't. They have no ears to hear this scratching sound but they feel the vibrations coming up through their legs from the surface of the soil (Spangler 1967). The sound is produced when the ant rubs two plates together, one on the last segment of the waist and the other on the first segment of the gaster, the part of the ant that follows the waist. Melander observed these scraping vibrations among red harvester ants trapped in a bottle. Oddly, neither McCook nor Lincecum mentioned stridulation during their extensive observations in the late nineteenth century, especially odd since they too studied the red harvester and since that scraping can be heard under quite casual conditions.

Worker harvesters on both continents stridulate. Other ants are attracted to the spot, but the function of the vibrations is controversial. Suggestions range from removal of soil particles (like an ultrasonic parts cleaner) to the assembly of a rescue detail for cave-ins at the mound. Two South American ants scrape their plates together. Marcus's harvester makes audible squeaks (Marcus and Marcus 1951) and *P. vermiculatus* stridulates as well.

Perhaps the most important function is part of the mating process. If so, then workers might be expected to inherit the ability whether it was useful to them or not. Stridulation by males and females in the huge mating swarms has two different functions. Males do it to end the confusion when one male attempts to mate with another (Markl, Hölldobler, and Hölldobler 1977). Females stridulate to signal the end of successful mating. These behaviors have been observed for rough, red, and Maricopa harvesters.

Something else borders on communication, although its ultimate function is unknown. Fire ants and harvesters are both attracted to electric fields. This has occasionally caused problems when cable insulation was ripped away by eager mandibles (MacKay et al. 1992).

Sex Life of the Harvester Ants

THE MATING SWARM

The alarm pheromone does double duty for the harvester ants. Its dispersal to the winds is also the summons for the amorous pandemonium of the mating ritual, which is indeed alarming in its size and frenzy (Hölldobler 1976b). Humans can detect the sweet smell of this perfume form of 4-methyl-3-heptanone from up to 50 feet away, and they can hear the buzzing of wings from the aerial armada (Michener 1948). Males issue the chemical summons when they arrive at the site and discharge the pheromone from their mandibular glands. It attracts not only females but an army of male competitors as well. The onset of mating at the lek is stimulated by a chemical in the female's poison gland. The familiar, wingless, nonreproductive worker ants have no role in this process except as a numerous and formidable guard to the sexuals as they erupt from the nest, bringing some of the houseguests out when they go.

Mating can occur several times per year per colony, but almost always in spring to early fall. Most species mate in the summer. Synchrony can be statewide; reports came in from all over

Oklahoma with descriptions of red harvester rituals that were sighted on a single day (Young and Howell 1954). The time of day varies depending upon the species. The Florida harvester begins in the morning while the red harvester chooses the afternoon (Lincecum 1866). Typically, they wait until a warm day following a rain when it is clear with little or no wind.

These congregations tend to occur at the same place year after year, and hundreds to thousands of individuals arrive from nests in the surrounding area. There is competition among males for mates as the sexuals arrive at the congregation site, or lekking ground. This is often a tree, a hilltop, or a cleared area on the ground. Florida harvesters and red harvesters mate on the ground, while the western ant settles on chimneys, grain elevators, and even the human head (Hungerford and Williams 1912). No harvester mates in the air, although that is the practice of the fire ant. The Florida species is unusual, in that mating is between brothers and sisters and that mating occurs on the surface of the nest with no prior flight (Harmon 1993). Inbreeding might be rather common among harvester ants (Cole and Wiernasz 1997), but the behavior of the red harvester ensures outbreeding because they fly to large open spaces or cleared areas on the ground before mating (Young and Howell 1954). The flying male of one South American species was graceful enough to be compared to a spider wasp (Bruch 1916). The only Comanche swarm on record was seen on a pecan tree, which it nearly covered with its bodies, so that mating clusters fell to the ground (Strandtmann 1942).

Males commonly form "sleeping clusters" after mating and die within a few days or return to the nest in the case of the Florida harvester. No one knows the fate of the returnees. Mated females fly and choose a site to begin digging the nest. Only one out of one thousand will survive the first season underground (Wildermuth and Davis 1931).

The details of sexual behavior among harvesters began appearing, often erroneously, in the literature just before and during the American Civil War. In 1859, a Texas state geologist named Samuel Buckley (1860) saw a July swarm of the red harvester. Buckley's reports were attacked in a paper by W. M. Wheeler (1902c) (as mentioned in the introduction). Buckley thought that workers help the newly fertilized females dig their first nest, but they do not. Gideon Lincecum (1866) was at his best in this department.

He saw a huge swarm (107 x 10 yards in area) with four to twenty males seeking to mate with each female, noted the flight of newly inseminated females, the removal of their wings upon beginning the nest, and the death of the spent males. These results have been corroborated by the natural historians that followed. One unique observation was the ascent of the males into vegetation, and the closure of their jaws on leaves or stems before death. This behavior hasn't been corroborated since, but similar behavior is known for parasitized arthropods.

The harvester ant arena was the first case of an insect lekking ground that could be compared to the more familiar examples from the vertebrate world, such as the strutting male sage grouse of the Great Plains (Hölldobler 1976b). Ironically, male sage grouse have been observed lekking on mounds and clearings of the western harvester ant (Giezentanner and Clark 1974).

Lincecum even counted the number of eggs laid by the new queen: twenty to thirty. We now know that these eggs are pearly white and round and tend to form little heaps. Each egg is a mere 0.5 millimeter in diameter (Lavigne 1969). Queens carry them about in their beard in the lab, but this has never been seen in nature. Tiny larvae hatch from the eggs, and after five to six weeks they will become adult workers by passing through several larval stages and the naked pupal stage (no cocoon is spun by the harvesters). Members of the first brood are typically small and are called "nanitic" (dwarfish). They open up the nest from the inside and the incipient colony begins its interactions with the rest of the world. Sexuals aren't produced until the colony is several years old, and the level of production is decreased when colonies are crowded together (Gordon and Wagner 1997).

THE MATING PROCESS

For many years after Lincecum there was almost no study of the harvester sex life, but the efforts of Wheeler and several living myrmecologists changed all that. We now know that stridulation plays an important role. Mating females make this scraping noise when they have had enough, and males stridulate to put a stop to homosexual encounters (Markl, Hölldobler, and Hölldobler 1977). Both sexuals commonly mate more than once and the female will have something like ten thousand sperm in the spermatheca—the organ in which sperm is stored—when mating is terminated (Johnson 1995) (see fig. 3.2). She will keep the sperm alive in this tiny organ for up to forty years, laying eggs for decades, but never mating again during the life of the colony.

The egg-laying queen produces sons and daughters. Two kinds of daughters exist, sterile workers and virgin queens. Each virgin queen will fly away to mate and start a nest of her own. Sterile workers stay home.

The whole mating process usually takes fifteen minutes or less, but insistent males are sometimes wounded by biting females, and queens have been observed with only the male's copulatory organs still attached, the remainder of her suitor quite missing. Sometimes the amorous male bites the female in half (Hölldobler 1976b). Males attempt to remove copulating males from their mates, and the whole process is accompanied by the buzzing of wings.

Hybridization has been observed or suspected between the rough and the red harvester, the rough and the western, the western and the red, and the western and the Maricopa (Nagel and Rettenmeyer 1973; Young and Howell 1964; Cole 1968; Ingham 1963). No such offspring have ever been raised. The reproductive behaviors of the two social parasites (Cole's harvester and *P. anergismus*) are unusual. Cole's harvester has no worker class and must live, as a parasite, off the efforts of its host colony, the rough harvester (Rissing 1983). Parasitized colonies are rare. Male parasites must mate with sisters because there is little chance of forming a successful lek as in the free-living harvesters. The mated female flies off and seeks a nest of a newly inseminated rough harvester. The pair live together (some ant parasites kill the host queen once a host worker force is established), but Cole's harvesters have a tough time getting accepted by colonies that already have a worker force in place. Such workers drag the invader out before she has a chance to begin laying eggs of her own.

A few species appear to have egg-layers that are something between a typical queen and the sterile worker caste with respect to body structure. These ergatogynes or intermorphs have been discovered in nests of *Ephebomyrmex imberbiculus* (Heinze, Hölldobler, and Cover 1992) and *P. huachucanus* (Cole 1968) in North America and in nests of Mayr's harvester, Marcus's harvester, *E. cunicularius, E. brevibarbis, P. longibarbis,* and *P. laticeps* of South America (Kusnezov 1951). Some never have wings and some have stubby wings. I discovered a rudimentary third eye in

what I had assumed was a series of Marcus's workers from Bolivia. These simple eyes or ocelli are always found in sexuals but
never in normal workers. Why so many unusual forms are found
in South America is a mystery, although there has been greater
opportunity to diversify in South America since the ants have lived
there longer than in North America. Sometimes we know that such
oddities are egg-layers *(E. imberbiculus),* but other times we must
simply infer, not having observed this behavior. Sometimes there is
more than just one *(E. imberbiculus),* but usually there is a single
presumptive "queen," whether or not she is strange looking. Males
can be odd too. William MacKay (1982b) discovered dimorphism
(existence of two size classes) in several North American harvesters, and the elongated head of Mayr's harvester has been described
as "freakish" (Kugler 1978).

The Harvesters Take a Physical

Ants are often used as examples of tiny but mighty animals that
can carry many times their own weight. This was the assessment
of H. C. McCook, who in 1882 described the red harvester as an
"emmet athlete." A harvester does a lot of toting as it forages but
a typical load is equal to its own weight or less. Still, it would be
quite unusual to see a two hundred–pound man lugging a two
hundred–pound burden on a regular basis. Foragers unencumbered
by any load have been clocked at 0.07 miles per hour.

Some species get started a little earlier in the morning than
others. The rough harvester is blackish and can warm up faster
than the more common red species (Bernstein 1971). A worker of
a large species, such as the rough harvester, measures almost half
an inch in length and tips the scale at 17 milligrams (Lighton and
Feener 1989). A more common weight would be about 6.5 milligrams, so that a 1-pound bag of ants would contain a writhing
mass of seventy thousand eager stingers or the equivalent of five
very large colonies. I have seen only the dry weight of a typical
larva and that is about 2 milligrams (Nielsen 1986). The queen of
the rough harvester can be as heavy as 48 milligrams, seven times
the weight of a typical harvester worker.

The water content of red harvesters is 50 percent in queens
and up to 67 percent in workers and males (Johnson, Parker, and
Rissing 1996). The egg-layer might be expected to have the least

amount of water because of the high percentage of fat needed for egg production. The queen's body is indeed about 40 percent fat, and her tissues have more calories than those of the other castes. The castes of *Pogonomyrmex subnitidus* survive the overwintering period by living off their own stored fat, not stored seeds (MacKay and MacKay 1984). At the low prevailing temperatures of western and midwestern American winters they might be too sluggish to feed on seeds anyway (ants are cold-blooded). Observations of *Pogonomyrmex salinus* show that workers and adult reproductive females overwinter, but males and juveniles do not. Overwintering is not a true state of hibernation (Cole 1934b), and in colder climes the queen will finally ascend from the snug depths in April or May (Lavigne 1969).

Are they sleeping down there all that time? Something like sleep has been reported on two occasions. First, the males of a mating swarm come together in clumps called "sleeping clusters" (Hölldobler 1976b). Perhaps this is a consequence of the higher metabolic rate they sustain just before the nuptial flight. Second, the big-headed major workers of the Florida harvester appear to sleep for several hours and even yawn upon awakening (McCook 1879). A caution here: this observation was made by one of the earliest pogo naturalists and it should be taken with a grain of salt. The farther back one goes into the literature, the greater the uncertainty of the results, although the writers might indeed be correct in their unique interpretations. In line with this is a report for Marcus's harvester of a statolith (mineral grains associated with the sense of balance) in an area known to contain the metapleural gland. No such organ has been reported in other ants.

Physiological experiments show that high-altitude ants consume more oxygen than lowlanders, and oxygen consumption is highest at high temperatures and at higher elevations (MacKay 1982b; Lighton and Bartholomew 1988). There are some exceptions. Foragers spend much time outside the protection of the nest, and under this exposure to predators and the elements they are expected to live from only a few weeks to a few months (Porter and Jorgensen 1980). They run a gauntlet of everything from bad weather to horned lizards to the crushing hooves of grazing mammals. Occasionally a human will catch up to one. Even a thundershower holds peril for an ant. The water could wash it away, remove physical and chemical trails, and destroy visual markers of the nest position. Aging workers lose weight and their teeth wear down to nubbins (Porter and Jorgensen 1981). These, as well as lean and unusually active ants, tend to live near the surface of the nest (they are more expendable). When these are injured or near death they leave the nest on their own (Wilson, Durlach, and Roth 1958).

Royalty has plenty of advantages, and greater life expectancy is among them. The queen lives deep underground and never leaves the nest once she begins to lay eggs. We have reliable figures for queen western harvester ages of forty years or more, perhaps the greatest life expectancy of any rangeland animal (Keeler 1993). It wasn't all that long ago that our own life expectancy and the maximum age of this insect were about equal. The large mammals that thunder overhead on the plains will be lucky to live that long. The biology of harvesters allows us to be confident of this number because colonies have only one queen and she is not replaced when she dies. With the short worker lifetimes all activity would cease within a few months. Individual mounds have been followed over time and distance (since they occasionally move about), giving us minimum ages of the queen.

The rough harvester is one of the species living in the hotter deserts. The permeability of the queen's exoskeleton is the lowest ever reported for an ant (Lighton et al. 1993). Low permeability is linked to desiccation resistance (ability to withstand dry conditions) and is expected in an animal that must prevent too much water loss across its exoskeleton as it looks for a nesting site in the desert summer. The western harvester can withstand the drying effects of laboratory Drierite desiccant for two days with little mortality. When heated in an oven it can withstand temperatures of 151°F if removed within one minute (Nagel 1971). These results are especially interesting when one realizes that the ants choose humidities of 100 percent over all lesser values when tested in the lab.

The red harvester has two additional adaptations. The body fluid has a high osmotic pressure (high solute concentration, in contrast to a high water concentration), and the spiracle valve (a partition that seals off breathing tubes from the outside world) is unusually complex (Mangrum 1954). These are thought to help the ant retain its water under conditions like those found in the desert. It's easy to overlook the need for adaptations against *low* temperatures, but desert nights can be very cold. Temperatures of about

40°F stop movement and eventually kill the ant (Whitford and Ettershank 1975). Harvester defenses against this extreme appear to be more behavioral than structural. The foragers will remain in the nest or return to it as the thermometer drops.

The California harvester metabolism appears to have a unique adaptation that could be linked to its diet of seeds. Its muscles burn lipids for energy instead of the carbohydrates typically burned by most other animals. Martin and Lieb (1979) noted that seeds are richer in lipids than in carbohydrates, and they suggested the link between special diet and their novel finding. The metabolism of the other harvesters might be similar but no one has looked into it. At least three species are known to have an enzyme (chitinase) in their gut that allows them to break down the exoskeletons of the other insects they feed upon (MacKay 1981).

An artificial nest in the laboratory, designed as an arena for observing ant behavior, can be stocked with a wide variety of individuals from various castes and nests. For example, such a nest could contain unmated females collected from the field and worker sisters from that same natural nest. Laboratory experiments have revealed circadian (daily) activities of harvesters. They will be found in the exposed area of an artificial nest at certain times of day, running about. These rhythms are broken when the gyne—the sexual female—mates (McCluskey 1992). The spectrum of daily activities is then reduced and this is expected when one realizes that her sole function in the colony will be to lay eggs underground.

Workers of the rough harvester learn more slowly than other foraging ants tested, but they don't forget as readily (Johnson, Rissing, and Killeen 1994). Information even exists on brain size, due to some microdissections performed in the 1920s (Pandazis 1930). Most *Pogonomyrmex* harvesters are bigger than *Ephebomyrmex* harvesters, and that is certainly true when *P. coarctatus* (the biggest of all) is compared to *E. naegelii* (one of the smallest). The first is many times larger than the second, but its brain is only twice as big (0.02 mm³ vs. 0.01 mm³). It would take about one hundred million harvester ant brains to fill that 1-liter bottle. Comparisons of intelligence are sometimes made by comparing the *relative* sizes of the brain. In that case, ephebos might be considered smarter than pogos, but that decision would be questioned when the complexities of their behaviors in the wild were compared. And is the red harvester smarter than the rough? It can certainly remove marking paint applied by human observers. The rough ant cannot (Whitford, Johnson, and Ramirez 1976).

I did some brain dissections when I used the cells of that organ to study the chromosomes of the North American harvesters (Taber, Cokendolpher, and Francke 1988) (figs. 5.1, 5.2, 5.3). I discovered not only great constancy within most available species but great constancy between species as well. *Pogonomyrmex* workers have thirty-two chromosomes per cell except for *P. huachucanus,* which has thirty-six. The number for *Ephebomyrmex imberbiculus* is much greater (fifty-eight to sixty-two), and it was the only case of variability within a sex. Male ants, bees, and wasps typically have half the number of chromosomes of the female. In line with this, I found sixteen chromosomes per cell in male pogos and thirty per cell in the single male *Ephebomyrmex* that I collected during the study.

We often hear that the cockroach will be one of the few survivors of nuclear catastrophe. Perhaps. Or perhaps harvester ants will instead be scavenging their dead, mutated bodies from the desert soil. A triple advantage makes the harvester colony one of the hardest of living targets for a nuclear attack (Cadwell 1973). Picture the queen 10 feet underground, never leaving the nest, and monopolizing the reproductive role. If such an attack were to come when the colony was beginning its overwintering period, not even the foragers would have to leave for several months. Studies with gamma radiation have shown even the unprotected ant to be pretty tough. Tunneling California harvesters slow down their activities

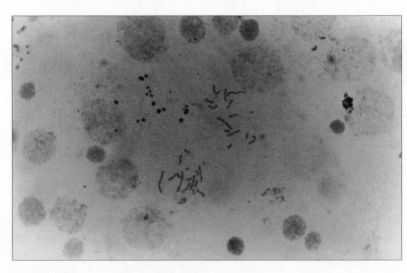

5.1 Chromosomes from the brain of a male harvester ant (P. barbatus). There are sixteen chromosomes in each nucleus of each cell.

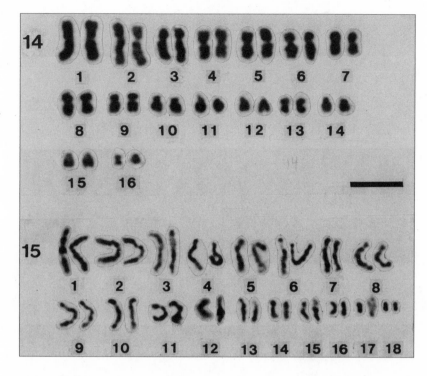

5.2 Karyotype (arranged chromosomes) of Pogonomyrmex subnitidus (upper) and P. huachucanus (lower). Scale line = 5 micrometers. (Reprinted from Taber et al. 1988. By permission of Birkhäuser Verlag AG.)

but do not cease burrowing underground until they face doses of 156,000 roentgens (Krebs and Benson 1966). The western harvester survives radiation that kills the plants surrounding its nest (Cadwell 1973). As a comparison, X-ray dosages of 3,000 roentgens (or less) during eight treatments (or less) have been linked to human leukemia when radiation was used against spinal rheumatoid arthritis (Morgan and Turner 1973).

Freaks and Giants

In 1866, Gideon Lincecum watched as the severed head of a red harvester moved about on its two antennae, as if they were feet. This nightmare lasted eighteen hours. Surprisingly few mutations and curious individuals are known among the harvesters.

As mentioned above, some species have a queen somewhat between the usual type and the worker in body shape. There is a whole slew of technical terms for such conditions, ergatogyne being most commonly used (ergato refers to workerlike, gyne to queenlike).

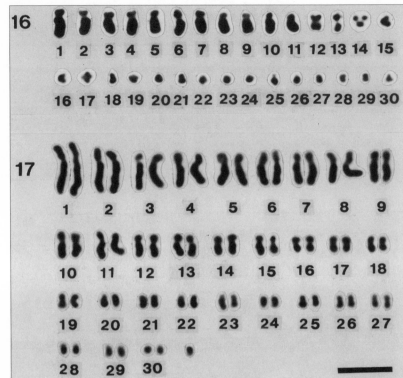

Something akin to it involving only the worker class is the phenomenon of polymorphism. A polymorphic species is one that has both large and small workers, the larger ones typically having heads that are proportionately even larger. The giant type is called a major, and majors of polymorphic harvesters might be specialized as seed processors or millers, rarely if ever leaving the nest to forage. Surprisingly, this hypothesis has not been firmly established or rejected by now.

Only one North American species is strongly polymorphic (the Florida harvester) and the same is true for South America *(P. coarctatus)*. Four ants from the southern continent are only weakly polymorphic. Their major workers do not have the outsized heads of the other two but there is clearly a group of larger individuals. These four species are *P. lobatus, P. bruchi, P. micans,* and *P. marcusi.* There are reports of giants among a sixth South American species (*P. vermiculatus*; Goetsch 1932). All of the workers of Marcus's harvester that I have seen have a third eye in the forehead like that usually restricted to the winged females and males.

True mutations are even more curious. Dr. Oscar Francke discovered a gynandromorph—part male, part female—of the western harvester while we were excavating a huge gravel mound in New Mexico (Taber and Francke 1986). Hundreds of ants were rushing over our feet but he picked out one winged ant because of its odd combination of colors. It had the dark color expected of a male as well as the orange color of a typical female. We observed it under a microscope and dissected the abdomen. The right side was male but the left side was female and each half was colored accordingly (fig. 5.4). Because male heads are smaller than females and their jaws and antennae look quite different, the resulting asym-

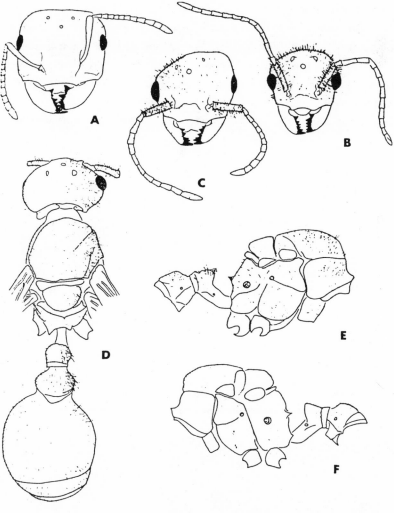

5.4 A gynandromorphic western harvester ant. A. Head of normal female. B. Head of normal male. C. Head of gynandromorph. D. Dorsal view. E. Right side of thorax. F. Left side of thorax. (Reprinted from Taber and Francke 1986. By permission of the Southwestern Association of Naturalists.)

metry gave the head a skewed look. We don't know if the beast functioned as one sex or the other or even if it was fertile.

Similar anomalies have been found among California harvesters and *P. salinus*. Males usually have antennae (feelers) with thirteen segments, but one batch of rough harvesters was discovered with only twelve (Emery 1921). Workers or workerlike ants with one or two pairs of wings are sometimes seen among Maricopa, Apache, Comanche, and California harvesters, as well as *P. subnitidus* and *P. texanus*. Harlow Shapley (1920a,b), the famous astronomer, was an amateur myrmecologist, and he was the one who found the winged California harvesters as he walked to and from an observatory. It's surprising that no such cases are known for the three most intensively studied species: the red, western, and Florida harvesters.

Mutations and abnormalities of the sterile workers seem to occur mostly in the abdomen. The spines and the waist are especially prone to being misshapen. Strange spines have been seen on the backs of the Maricopa, red, Florida, California, and Wheeler's harvester. Warped waist regions have been seen on workers of the Maricopa and California harvesters as well as on *P. salinus* (Cole 1968).

Chapter 6

Evolution and Diaspora

What evolutionary history is hidden within those quartz covered mounds!

—E. L. JOHNSTON, 1912,
ON THE WESTERN HARVESTER ANT

This chapter reports the results of my own research on the evolution and biogeography of the harvester ants. Evolution here means the origin of new species over millions of years, probably about sixty million years for the harvesters. Biogeography is the study of the movement and geographic distribution of living things. In other words, the study of where they live and how they got there.

There are two ways to account for the present distribution of harvester ants: dispersal (marching overland) and vicariance (division by geographic barriers). It now appears that the harvester ants arose in northern South America and moved through Central America on their way to the United States and southern Canada. There were three major diversions on this path. First, some *Ephebomyrmex* were carried into the Caribbean on what is now the island country of Haiti as it moved eastward after breaking away from Central America. Second, the pogos sent one wave into the western United States. Third, they sent a second small contingent into the eastern United States. Many species evolved from the

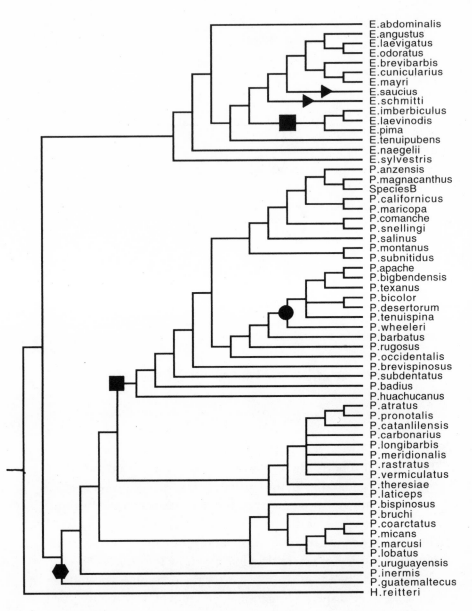

6.1 *The phylogeny or evolutionary tree of the harvester ants. The two social parasites have no worker caste and were therefore excluded from this analysis. Their phylogenetic position is approximated by the circle within the* P. barbatus *species complex. See figure 6.11 for a more detailed estimation of their position in the phylogeny.*

Symbols indicate the geographic distribution of all species that appear at or above that point in the majority rule consensus tree:

■=*North America,* ▲=*Haiti,* ⬟ =*Guatemala and southern Mexico*
No symbol = South America

western wave, but only the Florida harvester remains of the eastern diaspora. The ephebos of the United States are southwestern species only.

In both North and South America, harvester ants evolved with their homes in the grasslands, mountains, and deserts. The evidence for this scenario comes from the evolutionary tree of the harvester ants that I worked out using all sixty species and eighty-one anatomical and behavioral characteristics (fig. 6.1). (These characters are listed in appendix 3, as are the relevant tables.)

I provide the results here, but an explanation of the method would be out of place. There are many ways to reconstruct evolutionary patterns. I chose the best one, a cladistic method, and a standard computer analysis of the data set (Swofford 1993). Cladistic methodology is both rigorous and repeatable, properties highly desirable in any scientific method. In cladistics, one groups relatives by the possession of shared, derived characteristics. If you are interested in how one goes about this sort of thing, you will find a basic treatment of the subject in most modern introductory biology textbooks. Characters 82 through 97—ecology, behavior, nest structure, and habitat—were of the most interest to me, so I did not build the evolutionary tree with them. I "mapped" them onto the final product, the phylogeny or evolutionary tree, and inferred their evolution afterwards. Some authors believe that it is circular reasoning to build a tree with one set of characters and then to infer their evolution from that very result. My approach addresses that concern.

When you look at the evolutionary tree, you will see *H. reitteri* (fig. 6.2) just above the base or root. This is a close relative of the harvesters, and it was included to provide a frame of reference so that the evolution of anatomy, behavior, and ecological characters could be determined. The root of an evolutionary tree is the oldest part, representing the origin of the harvester ants (and the outgroup, or closest relative, *Hylomyrma*) in this case. First I will summarize the origin and dispersal of the harvesters, including such events as the origin of the Andes and Rockies and how that affected the evolution of the insects. Then I will summarize the evolution of the most interesting aspects of harvester biology and anatomy.

A comparison of the evolutionary tree of the harvesters and the geological and ecological events of the New World reveals a

6.2 Hylomyrma reitteri *from the jungles of South America is a little-known and rarely collected species.*

close correlation that might amount to cause and effect. The ages of deserts, grasslands, mountains, and rivers were determined by others, independent of my own work with the ants. The results are satisfyingly consistent with one another.

Origins of North American Harvesters

Species that branch off at the top of the tree are likely to be the most recent ones. I'll start there, with the most recent of the familiar North American harvesters, and work down to the origin of them all, about sixty million years ago in northwestern South America. It is convenient to work backward because we are more confident of recent geological events than of very old ones.

The hottest deserts of the western United States are clearly newcomers on the ecological scene, arriving within the last three million years or so (Elias and Van Devender 1992). If this is true, then we should expect the ants that live there to be new as well. And most of them are, branching off near the top of the tree. For example, the California and Maricopa harvesters, and *P. magnacanthus* and *P. anzensis,* dwell in great heat. The same is true for the desert harvester and to a lesser extent the Apache and *P. texanus* (figs. 6.3, 6.4).

A little further back in time is the uplift of the Rocky Mountains, an event that produced an arid rainshadow on the eastern slopes and allowed those hot deserts to begin expanding (Snelling

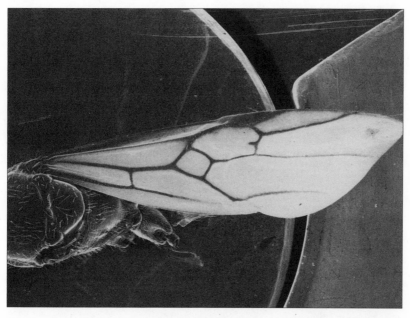

6.3 The fore-wing of a queen Pogonomyrmex texanus *(scanning electron micrograph). The queen caste was unknown until the author found it in Buddy Holly Park, Lubbock, Texas.*

and George 1979). Harvesters that lived when the Rockies began rising were not as well adapted to hot climates, which isn't surprising, because hot deserts hadn't appeared yet. The red harvester is one of these and it is older than the several species listed above. Yet another independent source of evidence corroborates this time interpretation of the evolutionary tree. Radioactively dated harvester ant fossils from packrat garbage piles show that the red harvester has been out west longer than the desert harvester, the Apache, and *P. texanus* (MacKay and Elias 1992). Even further

6.4 The author collecting P. texanus *by using an aspirator. (Photo taken by Mark Rogers and used with the permission of Joe Don Buckner, Lubbock Avalanche-Journal.)*

back is the origin of North American grasslands (Pflieger 1971) and the western harvester whose mounds still pepper the Great Plains. A more conventional fossil from central Colorado (fig. 6.5) suggests that harvesters of some kind were there thirty million years ago when conditions were actually swampy (Burnham 1978).

This takes us to the most interesting North American problem, the origin of the Florida harvester. It looks strange to begin with, but its distribution is even stranger. It is found east of the Mississippi River and nowhere else; all other harvesters are confined to the western side of that formidable barrier. The Florida harvester or an immediate ancestor probably originated with the eastern of the two colonization waves into the modern United States, about twenty-five million years ago. The southward extension of the Mississippi River cut across the area (Nelson 1988), isolating the Florida harvester or its ancestors within the last five million years or so. The Mississippi is difficult to cross, and the unusual mating ritual might have something to do with the insect's isolation. The female Florida harvester does not fly before mating, which reduces the distance of dispersal, compared to a typical western species, such as the red harvester. There is additional evidence that the biota of eastern and western North America were isolated from one another by one or more events of roughly Miocene age. For trees, this isolation might have been caused by a central arid re-

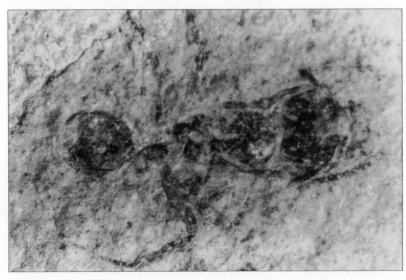

6.5 Ephebo-myrmex fossilis *(dorsal view) from the Oli-gocene of Flo-rissant National Monument, Colorado. The remains of this ant are thirty million years old.*

gion (Berry 1923). For the harvesters, the barrier was probably different, mesic conditions or bodies of water.

The real relict or greybeard of this huge twenty-six-species North American group appears to be the Huachuca harvester, *P. huachucanus*. It is found in the Huachuca Mountains of southern Arizona and in the surrounding area where it is only spottily distributed. It is small for a pogo, has an unusual anatomy, and is the only species known to have thirty-six chromosomes instead of thirty-two. Something much like this one was the ancestor of the two waves that entered the United States and Mexico about thirty million years ago. The gradually shrinking tropical dry forest of western Middle America might have provided that corridor (Crowe 1997), for the present intercontinental connection of the harvesters is closely linked to it by the presence of *P. wheeleri* along the western coast of Mexico. These are the trends that I see for the most familiar of the harvesters. However, the really interesting biogeography lies in South America, where the very first harvester came onto the scene.

Origins of the South American Harvesters

Once again it is easier to work backward in time because our most reliable information is about the most recent events. Mayr's harvester is a good place to start. This is the weirdest looking of all. It has a restricted distribution in the mountains, rather like the Huachuca ant in this regard. However, it is not a relict. The phylogeny suggests that *E. mayri* is recent and its home in the Santa Marta Mountains of northwestern Colombia was probably underwater until just a few million years ago (Murphy and Lugo 1995). The northern Andes are indeed the youngest part of the range. The present-day Amazon rain forest is probably of similar age. Its growth was the vicariance event that split one large, ancestral population into two, resulting in the evolution of Mayr's harvester in the north and *E. cunicularius* in the south. These two are closest relatives (sister species).

The Amazon rain forest is a center of species diversity, a lush paradise for untold numbers of creatures but not for the harvesters. Only Naegeli's harvester *(E. naegelii)* lives in these humid jungles. Sometime about twenty to thirty million years ago the central and southern Andes rose and produced an arid desert region on the eastern slopes (Rundel 1981). Harvesters speciated in concert with this, much as they did in the deserts of North America. A few species were left on the western, coastal side of the new chain. One of them lived in the Southern Beech and monkey puzzle (Norfolk Island Pine) forests where a trio of its descendants live today. This is an unusual habitat for harvesters. The famous pampas grasslands evolved in the east, on the coattails of the arid regions (Baez and Yane 1979), and they were colonized by most of today's polymorphic species. *Pogonomyrmex coarctatus,* the biggest of all the harvesters, is a pampas ant.

The origin of the island of Hispaniola and therefore of Haiti is still deeper back in time and just how and when that happened remains controversial. It appears that it broke away from Central America tens of millions of years ago (Murphy and Lugo 1995). When it did, it moved eastward, into the Caribbean, taking the ancestor(s) of *E. saucius* and *E. schmitti* with it. These two tiny ants with their small and fairly uncommon colonies probably originated in this way. Dispersal from the mainland on a natural raft seems less likely.

Next we jump all the way back to the origin of the first harvester ant. The forest was its ancestral home, as it is for *E. sylvestris* (fig. 6.6) today. Note that this ant arises very near the base or root of the evolutionary tree. This probably happened fifty or sixty million years ago at the end of the dinosaur age when the world was becoming drier. The living species might be this old, or per-

6.6 Perhaps the most primitive living harvester. This is the holotype of Ephebomyrmex sylvestris *from the jungles of Venezuela.*

haps some ancestors are now extinct, leaving only this remnant of an ancient branch.

Why do I think the harvesters are so old? Myrmecologists agree that harvesters are a primitive type, but that alone is not enough, and we certainly don't have their fossils from this time. They're considered so old because (1) the region was arid enough by that time to support ants that do well in dry habitats (Gentry 1982; Gillis 1996), (2) we *do* have fossils of ants from thirty million years ago that appear to be of a more recent type than the harvesters (more "highly evolved") (Hölldobler and Wilson 1990), and (3) ants are famous for their slow rates of evolution. Some ants living today are hardly distinguishable from thirty-million-year-old fossils. An example is the big black carpenter ant that can be seen running up and down tree trunks and along the walls of houses. Some of these look just like ants that can be clearly seen inside transparent Baltic amber of early Oligocene age, although the carpenters are not even primitive among the ants. Molecular evidence indicates an even greater age than the fossil evidence. Mitochondrial DNA sequences suggest that ants arose in the early Jurassic, 185 million years ago (Crozier, Jermiin, and Chiotnis 1997).

Before the origin of Haiti it is hard to correlate geological or ecological events with events on the evolutionary tree. However, note how far up in the tree the two Haitian species, *E. saucius* and *E. schmitti,* arise. Harvesters were already old by that time, which might well have been about thirty million years ago. Note that there has been no mention of the celebrated Pliocene land bridge that connected North and South America several million years ago. When that connection was made, allowing massive mammalian migration in both directions, the harvester dispersal was already ancient history.

The oldest living pogo is perhaps *P. guatemaltecus* (fig. 6.7), which arises from the base of the *Pogonomyrmex* clade. Its status as a relict is reinforced by its isolated and limited distribution, for it is known from only a few nests. As the only Central American species, it is the central or middle element of the entire harvester clan. On one side are the North American species, on the other side are the South American species. A considerable mileage gap in both instances further underscores the isolation of *P. guatemaltecus.* How did this ant come to occupy such a strange position on the map? The answer seems to be connected with the

6.7 An evolutionary enigma. The Guatemala harvester is an isolated relict with a central distribution, between the North American and South American species.

separation of North America from South America in the Cretaceous. That fracture line ran right through the modern range of *P. guatemaltecus,* in the region of southern Guatemala (see diagram in Strickberger 1996). There is some cause and effect here, or an uncanny coincidence. More than one mystery lies in the heartland of the Maya.

The origin and dispersal of the harvester ants is summarized in figure 6.8. The inset shows a similar pattern for a group of gall wasps (Ross 1973), and a comparison of the two suggests that we're on the track of real historical dispersal events that affected whole groups of organisms.

After identifying northwestern South America as the likely homeland of the harvesters, and the Guatemalan area of Central America as the possible homeland of *Pogonomyrmex* in particular, I discovered that both areas were identified by Croizat (1958) as especially important centers of dispersal for a wide variety of organisms. These regions were named the Guiana Foreland and Nuclear Central America, respectively. The arid forelands arose in the Cretaceous, which coincides both with my own ideas for the age of the harvester ants and with the preferred climate type of most living species. Both time and place of origin coincide closely with the asteroid impact that might have put an end to the dinosaurs. This could explain the unusual disjunction between the relict *P. guatemaltecus,* which arose near the suspected impact site in the

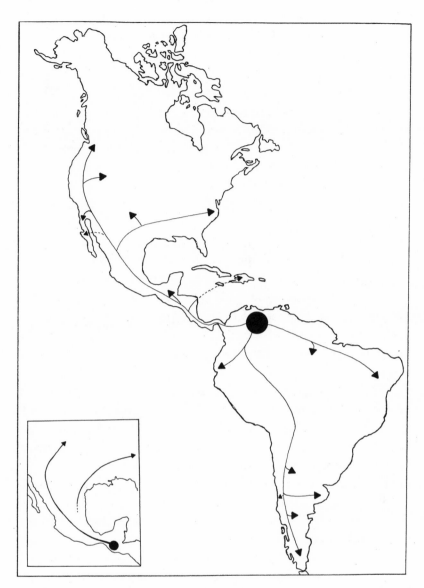

6.8 The origin and dispersal of the harvester ants from the forests of northern South America. Dashed lines indicate distributions due to land mass separation, not to dispersal over water. The inset shows a similar pattern for gall wasps discovered by A. C. Kinsey. (Inset adapted from the History of Entomology © 1973 by Annual Reviews.)

Yucatan, and the other harvesters of a similar age. The effect of the Cretaceous impact on any nearby ants and on dinosaurs in general is unclear.

Ant Behaviors and Bodies

Please note that the following summary does not consider the two social parasites since they lack a worker caste. The generalizations are all based upon a rigorous mathematical interpretation of the phylogeny (character-optimization procedures, procedures for figuring out the best way to interpret the evolution of ant characteristics).

The first harvester, presumably long extinct, was the common ancestor of both *Pogonomyrmex* and *Ephebomyrmex*. It probably lacked a beard, but we can't be as sure about its diet until we know more about the food of living *Ephebomyrmex* species, particularly *E. sylvestris* from the Venezuelan jungles. We know more about pogos than ephebos for the same reasons that we know more about cattle than wombats. Pogos are more conspicuous and have at least some economic importance. Accordingly, the evolutionary tree suggests that the first pogo probably had a beard and a strong taste for seeds. It was using that beard as an earthmover, and it was collecting those seeds in the newly evolving grasslands of northern South America or Central America. The living Guatemalan species might be a relict of that primitive condition. The beard must be a good adaptation, for the pogo worker caste never lost it.

There was a reduction in the size of the beard in the Huachuca harvester and in the ancestor of *P. bispinosus* of Chile. The South American pampas ants and the others that descended from that ancestor retain that smaller beard today. If a reduction did occur anywhere among the harvesters, we might expect it to occur more often among such grassland species than among sandy desert dwellers, since a shovel, like the beard-basket, is more useful for scooping up loose sand than packed turf. Pogos come from a lineage with strong beards. Thus, pogos with small beards and those that do not have a strong preference for seeds are probably not *retaining* a primitive condition; they have gone *back* to that condition. Ironically, their apparently primitive states are quite modern. I might not have guessed this without an evolutionary tree as the basis for analysis. One thing seems clear enough; the harvester beard is conspicuous for its lack of variability within each species.

The first ephebo probably lacked a beard, as its descendants do today, with one arguable exception in the form of *E. brevibarbis*. But even here the name suggests a short goatee. It's not clear if the first ephebo had a strong preference for seeds or if it was more nearly carnivorous. Someone should look inside the nests of the South American species in particular, in the storage chambers, so that these data can be mapped onto the phylogeny and analyzed to determine the primitive state.

Gideon Lincecum seems to have been quite perceptive about the evolution of the harvester diet. He suggested to Darwin that pogos had evolved from hunters to aphid-tenders and then to seed-eaters over the course of millions of years (Burkhalter 1965). Jones (1929) later observed the western harvester taking honeydew from an aphid, and although this is a single record and not quite "tending," everything else is supported by the phylogeny and the fossil record.

In a number of ants, the distinct clypeal lobes of the facial area (see fig. A2.1) have experienced a great deal of historical change. Santschi (1921) opined that these lobes might be defensive structures that protect the antennae during combat, but the present results don't seem to support that. Some fighters lack them, some timid types possess them, and their development occasionally increases when the diet takes a granivorous turn.

The evolution of the teeth shows more uniformity and would please those who embrace the quasimystical concept of "orthogenesis." Orthogenesis ascribes a purpose to historical change, usually the attainment of perfection. There has indeed been a trend to increase the number of teeth in the jaw. This might increase the food-handling efficiency of the workers. Furthermore, a reversal to a primitive, reduced tooth number among North American pogos has occurred only twice—once in *P. bigbendensis* and again in *P. anzensis*. Both ants are unusually rare. Their lack of success might be related to this reversal or to some other feature correlated with the reduction in tooth number.

Polymorphism has also been linked to diet. Oster and Wilson (1978) suggested that the absence of competition from other seed specialists might bestow "ecological release" on ants, which could then begin varying the worker size class in a way that more efficiently uses the abundant resources. The harvester phylogeny supports that hypothesis. Polymorphism arose twice, in both cases on the relatively mesic eastern half of a continent, where seed specialists are less common than in the arid west. In North America, this happened to *P. badius*. In South America, it happened in the ancestor of the pampas clade that includes *P. coarctatus*.

Nest plugging and colony emigration appear to be primitive conditions for the harvesters, but there is a lack of data for many species. The most evolutionarily labile characters (those most prone to change) are those that describe the texture of the exoskeleton. This should be no surprise, because such traits might have little adaptive value. A few characters are conservative, arising only once over time, and staying in place thereafter. These include the diagnostic ventral seta, or hair, of the *P. barbatus* species group and the increase in segment number seen among the mouthparts of several *Ephebomyrmex* species. Since the setae appear to have no adaptive value, their further lack of evolutionary change is a surprise. The mouthpart change occurred in the ancestor of *E. angustus* in that strange Andean forest habitat of South America. I have no idea what adaptive value, if any, this has. It might be a case of "neutral" evolution. It violates Williston's Rule, which expects segments to reduce in number over time.

The complicated gravel mounds are limited to North American *Pogonomyrmex,* and they arose with the western harvester (or an immediate ancestor) and its grassland home. The aggressive stinging behavior first appeared about that same time. It is quite possible that the evolution of aggressive nest defense allowed the harvesters to spread out quickly over the newly colonized continent. This would be an example of adaptive radiation (the proliferation of species in a new habitat made possible by the origin of a new structure and/or behavior), with aggression as the key character that allowed the newcomers to expand into a vacant niche. Large colony size and group foraging are probably a little older, arising when the ants split into a western wave and an eastern wave. This would have coincided with the appearance of the Florida harvester.

There has also been a tendency for these insect species to increase in size over time, following a trend for vertebrate species like ourselves, which is called Cope's Rule (Grant 1985). This trend has produced cases of "gigantism" among the backboned animals and is sometimes seen as a sign of genealogical or racial senescence leading quickly to extinction. The tendency is not as prevalent among the invertebrates, although there are examples in the fossil record among clams, sea urchins, and the ammonites. I can at least say that the earliest harvesters were not the big ones. However, the big ones seem to be doing *better* than the little ones. If so, perhaps it is because large harvesters tend to have more young than small harvesters, whereas large mammals tend to have relatively few compared to small mammals. Cope's Rule is largely satisfied, but if there is any senescence, it is probably among the small harvesters. The smaller species are generally not as widespread, are uncommon within their limited ranges, and have very few individuals per colony.

The earliest harvesters had morning mating rituals up in the trees or on hilltops and mountains. Afternoon flights arose with the western harvester, but there were ground matings long before, appearing about the time of the Florida harvester. The species with sexuals only and with no worker class are the two social parasites (figs. 6.9, 6.10). They arose fairly recently from close relatives of the ants they parasitize, but they evolved at the same time from a single common ancestor, not on two separate occasions. The closest relative of each is therefore not a host species (fig. 6.11). This result falsifies the strictest interpretation of something called Emery's Rule (Hölldobler and Wilson 1990). According to that rule, the closest relatives of the parasites are their hosts. The placement of the parasitic species high up in the phylogeny also suggests that they have evolved recently.

The phylogeny can be used as a basis for the classification of the harvesters. In fact, such an evolutionary tree is a prerequisite for the proper, or at least ideal, classification of any organism, because monophyletic groups must be established first. It is easy to see why these complete or "natural" groupings of relatives are desirable for biological classification, because classification *follows* genealogy. A monophyletic or natural group is a portion or clade of a tree that contains an ancestor and *all* of its descendants, and nothing

6.9 *A social parasite and its host. Male (upper) and female (center)* of Pogonomyrmex anergismus. *At the bottom is a dark host worker of the rough harvester,* P. rugosus.

6.10 Another social parasite. Male (upper) and female (lower) of Pogonomyrmex colei. *The species has no worker caste. It lives in the nest of the rough harvester ant.*

more. The ancestor is usually hypothetical, but its position can be shown on the phylogeny as well. We don't want to leave any species out if they belong, and we don't want to add species that belong elsewhere in the tree. There has been no such phylogeny for the harvesters until now.

I recognize two genera, *Ephebomyrmex* and *Pogonomyrmex.* The first fork or bifurcation of the evolutionary tree shown in figure 6.1 (also the level of the nonharvester out-group *Hylomyrma*), is the branching point that defines the natural group that contains these two smaller natural groups. Some authors recognize each of the two as subgenera within the genus *Pogonomyrmex,* but others don't recognize even *this* distinction. Given the two monophyletic groups, why do I think each should be recognized as a genus? A glance at the illustrated genera of living ants in Hölldobler and Wilson 1990 shows at least a few recognized genera that look even less different from one another than do, say, *E. sylvestris* and *P. guatemaltecus.*

Furthermore, I considered this problem from a third, very different perspective provided by the chromosomes. All studied female pogos have either thirty-two chromosomes (most of those studied) or thirty-six *(P. huachucanus). Ephebomyrmex imberbiculus* has fifty-eight to sixty (sometimes a few more), almost twice as many as the pogos. This difference in number is more like those seen *among* genera of ants than within genera. There are bound to be exceptions to the rule that ants with such greatly different chromosome numbers belong to different genera. My results (seen in fig. 6.1) disagree somewhat with Cole's ideas on relationships within the harvester clan (1968); for example, the problematic, primitive, and relict North American species *P. huachucanus* and *P. guate-*

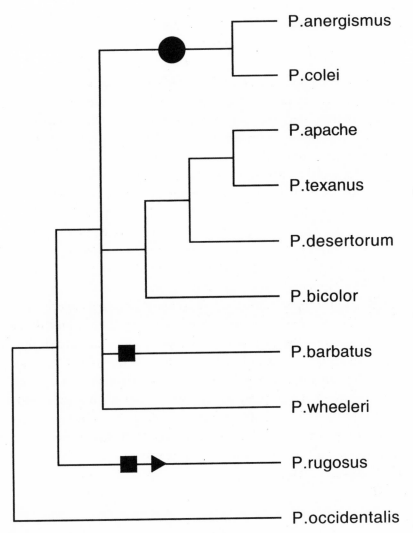

6.11 *The phylogeny of the social parasites. The single origin of social parasitism is indicated by a circle. Squares indicate hosts of* P. anergismus, *a triangle indicates the host of* P. colei. *All of these species are North American. This is a majority rule consensus tree.*

maltecus appear here as pogos, not as ephebos. The same is true for *P. bispinosus* of Chile.

Finally, let me explain a method that I did *not* use. I did not define *Ephebomyrmex* on the basis of one or more characters shared by all members. It is often believed that there must be some such special feature shared by all living members of a genus that can be used to define that genus. For example, if all members of *Ephebomyrmex* had a cocoon during development, we could use that to classify them as a distinct group of species. This assumption often fails when we actually determine the relationships of animals using all the data at hand. If *one* descendant of a cocoon-making ancestor loses that ability, the character can no longer be applied to *all* members of the genus.

For the harvesters, evolution has played havoc with the kinds of characters myrmecologists are familiar with, and there is no single, shared, derived trait that sets living ephebos apart from pogos. The pogos do indeed have their beards, and a flattened clypeal plate. That sets *them* apart from the primitive condition that preceded the harvester clan. But picture the first ephebo with any of the many traits that might have evolved at that point in time. Now picture all the descendants of that species, including those alive today. A single reversal to a primitive condition any-where in that family over the course of millions of years obviates that character as a single, defining trait for *all* ephebos. That is what has happened with each of the familiar characters. Such re-versals are forms of homoplasy (a similarity between species that is *not* due to inheritance from a common ancestor), and this is rampant among the insects. My own work with plant lice showed this with statistical rigor (Taber 1994). But there is possibly a good character out there somewhere for all living ephebos. The chro-mosome number has every indication of being such a trait, and I hope myrmecologists in South America will pick up the taxonomic and cytologic cudgels. There is still much to be discovered in the homeland of the harvester clan. The best way to classify them might be discovered there too.

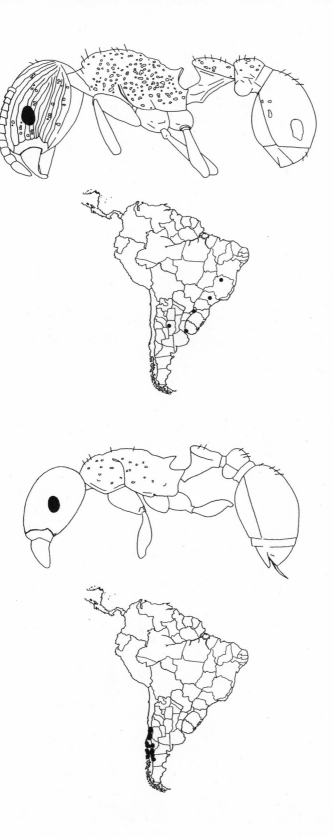

Ephebomyrmex
abdominalis.
*Reddish brown,
with a strongly
developed waist
region. Rarely
collected and
biology un-
known.*

Ephebomyrmex
angustus. *The
deep, jet-black
color of this ant
makes it
difficult to
capture much
detail in a
drawing.*

Ephebomyrmex brevibarbis. *A slender, black harvester with a sparse "beard" atypical of the genus, which normally bears only a few short hairs or setae under the head.*

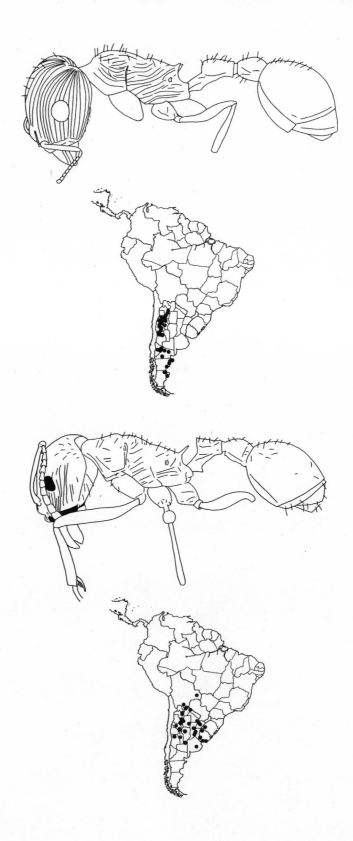

Ephebomyrmex cunicularius. *Formerly thought to be a pogo. Orange-red and large for its genus, it lives in a wide variety of habitats.*

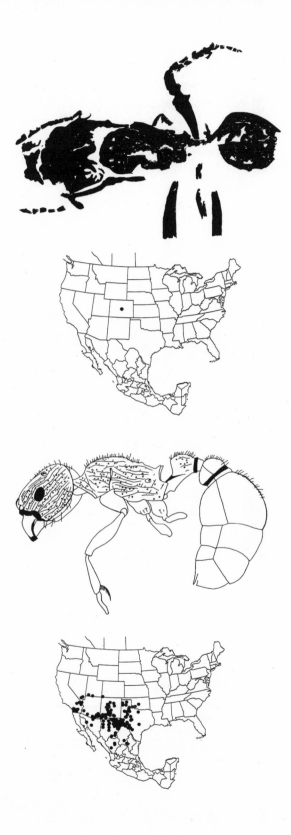

Ephebomyrmex fossilis. *An extinct species. This type specimen was dug from shale deposits in Florissant National Monument. It is thirty million years old.*

Ephebomyrmex imberbiculus. *Reddish brown and small. The most common North American ephebo, but encountered rarely enough at that.*

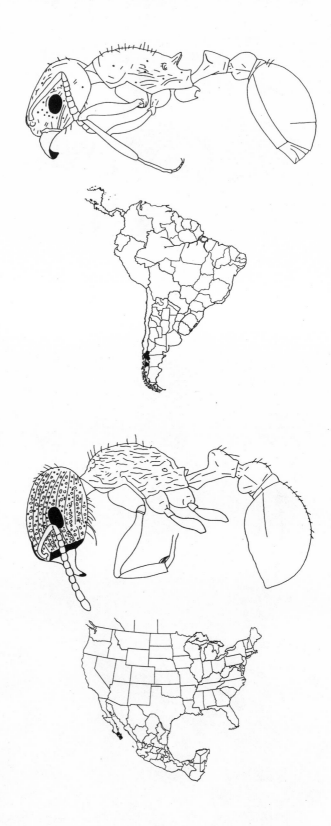

Ephebomyrmex
laevigatus. *A
black ant.
Biology almost
unknown.*

Ephebomyrmex
laevinodis.
*Yellowish red.
Little is known
about it.*

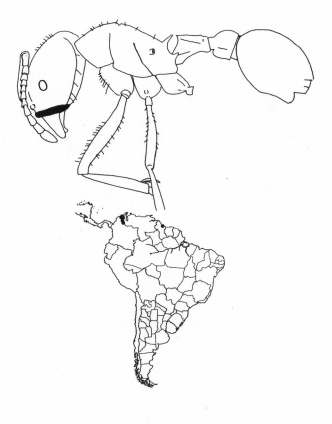

Ephebomyrmex mayri. *Black velvet and atypical in appearance. The Guyana record is a first, discovered among the ants of the Harvard collection. Mayr's harvester.*

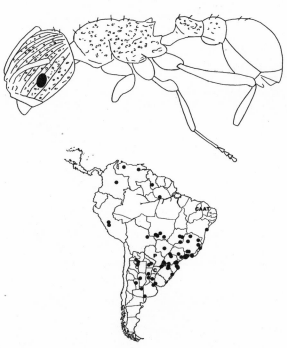

Ephebomyrmex naegelii. *The most widely distributed harvester. Reddish brown. The "P" on the map is an unspecified Paraguay record, the "C" is for the province of Corrientes, Argentina, and "CAAT" stands for "caatinga" (unspecified savanna record). Naegeli's harvester.*

97

Ephebomyrmex odoratus. *An unusual dark yellow color, with blackish blotches.*

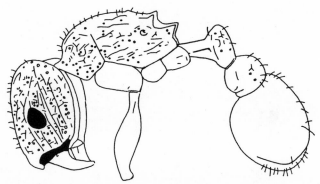

Ephebomyrmex pima. *Reddish brown. Easily confused with imberbiculus, but pima lacks the little pointed lobes below the antennae.*

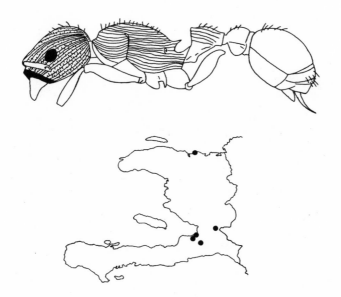

Ephebomyrmex
saucius. *One
of the two
Haitian harvest-
ers. Dark red-
dish brown
to blackish.*

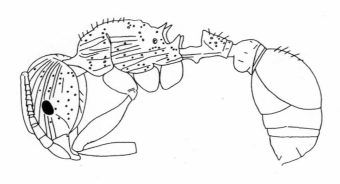

Ephebomyrmex
schmitti. *One of
the two Haitian
harvesters.
Dark reddish
brown to black-
ish. Schmitt's
harvester.*

Ephebomyrmex sylvestris. *A forest dweller with a primitive appearance. Shiny reddish brown. This is the holotype specimen. Almost nothing is known about this species.*

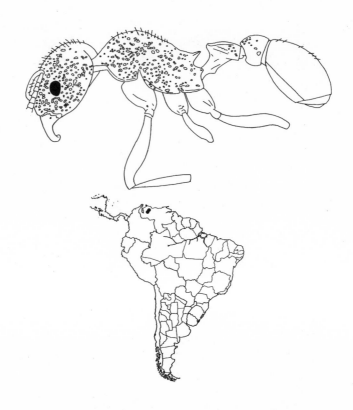

Ephebomyrmex tenuipubens. *Reddish brown with darker gaster. Rarely collected and biology unknown. This is one of the types.*

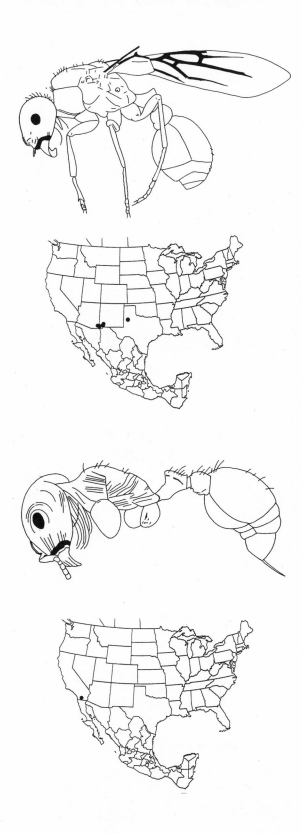

Pogonomyrmex anergismus. *One of the two social parasites. This is a queen; there is no worker caste. Rarely collected, not much known about its biology. Reddish brown. The wings of this type specimen are damaged but unimportant for identification.*

Pogonomyrmex anzensis. *Reddish brown. Collected only once; this is a type specimen. Note the famous sting of the harvester ants. The Anza Desert harvester.*

Pogonomyrmex
apache. *A large
species with
a small colony.
Red or brown-
ish red. The
Apache har-
vester.*

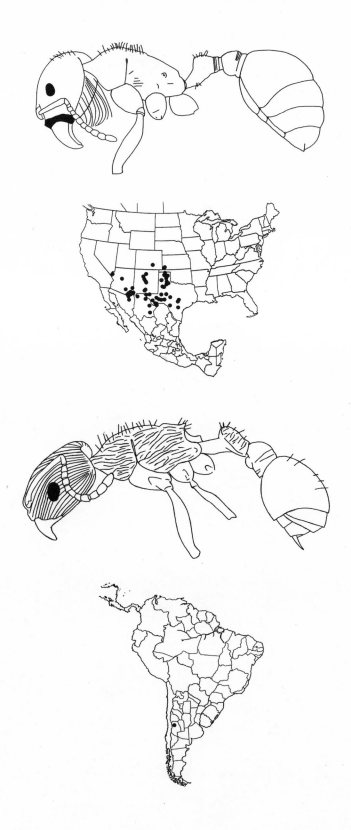

Pogonomyrmex
atratus. *A black
ant with an
unknown
biology.*

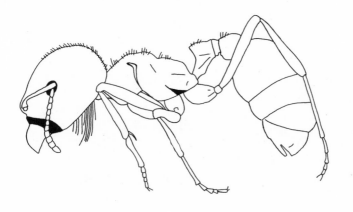

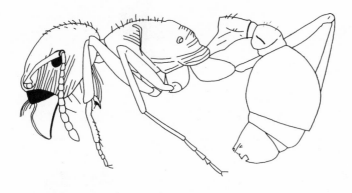

Pogonomyrmex badius. *Reddish brown. The only polymorphic harvester in North America. The top figure is a major worker, perhaps a seed processor or nurse. The bottom figure is a minor worker; this subcaste is more commonly seen than the major. The first harvester known to science (1802). The Florida harvester.*

103

Pogonomyrmex barbatus. *Lateral view, frontal view of head, and a larva. Reddish brown to red. Hence the name "red harvester."*

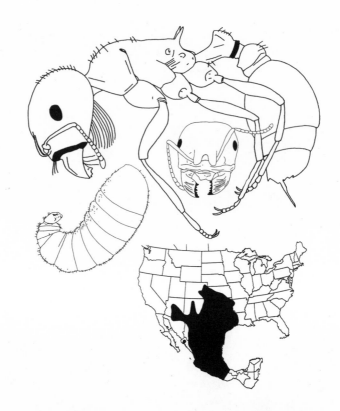

Pogonomyrmex bicolor. *The gaster is commonly blackish, while the rest is the usual reddish brown, hence the name. Biology poorly known.*

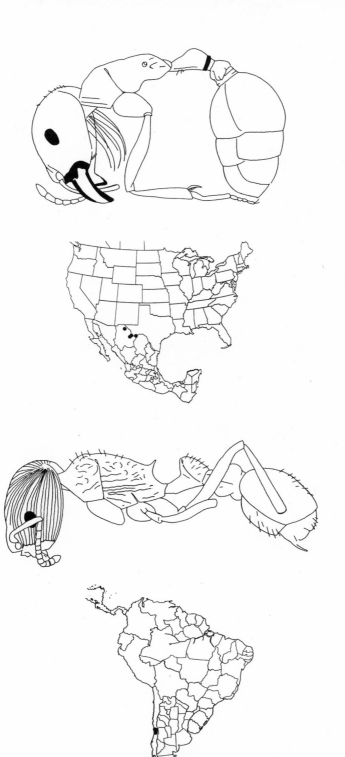

Pogonomyrmex
bigbendensis.
*Very light red
or yellowish.
Biology poorly
known. This is
a type speci-
men. The Big
Bend harvester.*

Pogonomyrmex
bispinosus.
*Brownish red.
Biology almost
unknown.*

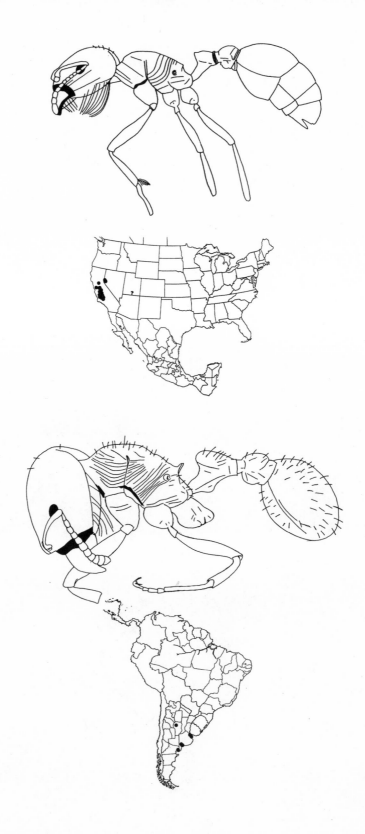

*Pogonomyrmex
brevispinosus.
A small, reddish
brown pogo.
The "?" on the
map refers to a
southern Utah
record that
couldn't be
pinned down.*

Pogonomyrmex
bruchi. *One of
the weakly
polymorphic
harvesters. Red.
Bruch's har-
vester.*

Pogonomyrmex
californicus.
*Reddish brown.
The "?" on the
map indicates
an unspecified
collection local-
ity in the Okla-
homa pan-
handle. The
California
harvester.*

Pogonomyrmex
carbonarius. *No
harvester has
been found
farther south.
Black. Biology
poorly known.*

Pogonomyrmex catanlilensis. *One of the prettiest harvesters. Black with a bright orange gaster. This is one of the types. Biology unknown.*

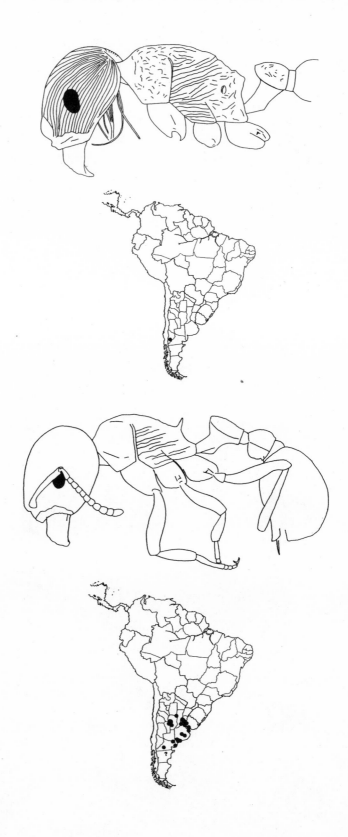

Pogonomyrmex coarctatus. *Red. The biggest harvester and the only strongly polymorphic species in South America. This is a major worker. The "?" on the map indicates an unspecified collection locality in the province of Chubut, Argentina.*

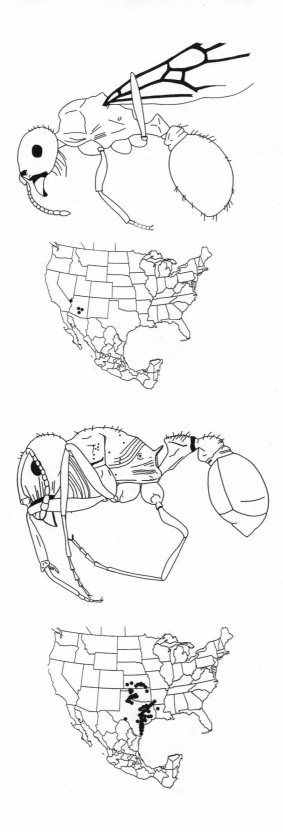

Pogonomyrmex colei. *One of the two social parasites. Dark reddish brown. Its biology has been worked out to some extent. This is a queen, one of the types. Cole's harvester.*

Pogonomyrmex comanche. *Reddish brown. Biology poorly known. The Comanche harvester.*

Pogonomyrmex
desertorum.
*Small and
reddish brown.
The "?" on the
map indicates
an unspecified
Oklahoma
collection local-
ity, and another
in the state of
San Luis Potosi,
Mexico. The
desert harvester.*

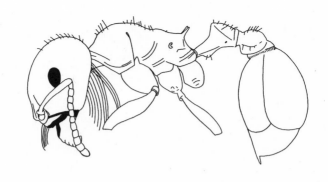

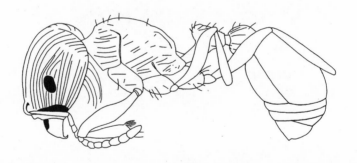

Pogonomyrmex
guatemaltecus.
*A small, reddish
brown ant with
all the earmarks
of a relict.
Biology poorly
known. The
Guatemala
harvester.*

Pogonomyrmex
huachucanus.
*Reddish brown.
Small, primi-
tive, and
relictual, like
the Guatemala
harvester. Biol-
ogy poorly
known. The "?"
on the map
indicates an
unspecified
record from the
state of Sonora,
Mexico. The
Huachuca
harvester.*

Pogonomyrmex
inermis. *Small
and yellowish
red with a
blackish gaster.
The "?" on the
map indicates
an unspecified
collection local-
ity in the prov-
ince of Rio
Negro, Argen-
tina.*

Pogonomyrmex
laticeps. *An
Andean ant
with variable
color.*

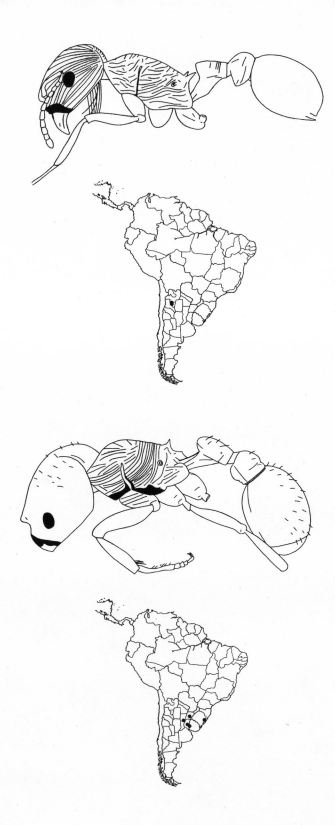

Pogonomyrmex
lobatus. *Red-
dish. One of
the weakly
polymorphic
South American
species.*

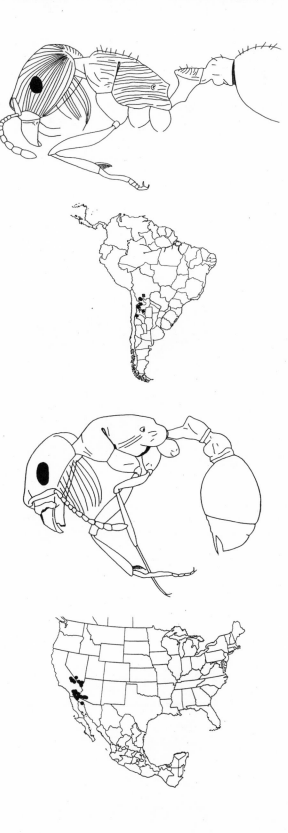

Pogonomyrmex longibarbis. *An Andean ant with variable color. The "?" on the map indicates an unspecified locality in the province of Catamarca, Argentina. The "B" indicates an unspecified Bolivian record. The long-bearded harvester.*

Pogonomyrmex magnacanthus. *Small, reddish brown. The big-eyed harvester.*

Pogonomyrmex marcusi. *One of the weakly polymorphic South American harvesters. Red. Marcus's harvester.*

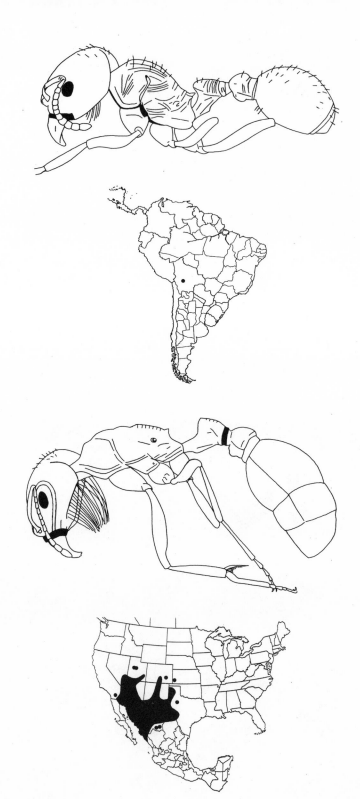

Pogonomyrmex maricopa. *Reddish brown. The loops around the eyes are exaggerated to illustrate a feature common to a particular species group of harvesters: rugae (wrinkles) of the exoskeleton, which form circumocular whorls. The Maricopa harvester.*

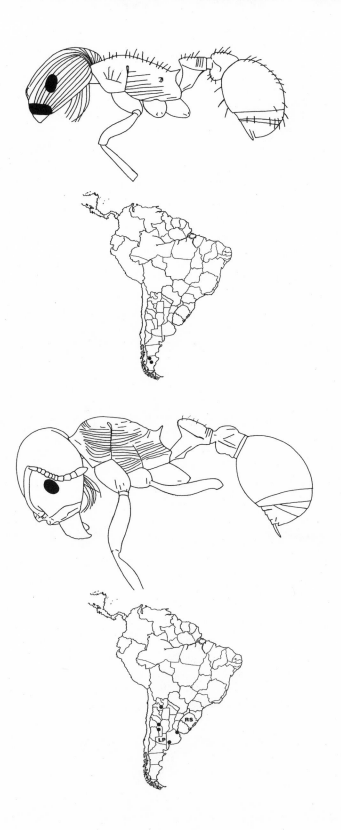

Pogonomyrmex
meridionalis.
*Color variable.
The southern
harvester of
South America.*

Pogonomyrmex
micans. *Red.
The "RS" on
the map indi-
cates an
unspecified
collection local-
ity in the state
of Rio Grande
do Sul, Brazil.
The "LP"
indicates an
unspecified
record from
the province
of La Pampa,
Argentina.*

Pogonomyrmex
montanus.
*Small for a
pogo and red-
dish brown.
The montane
harvester.*

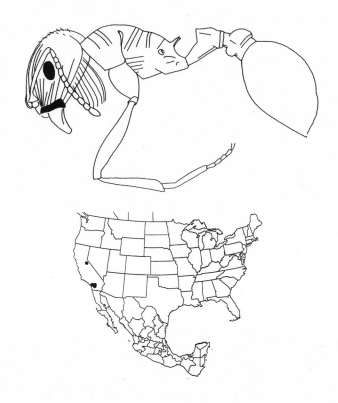

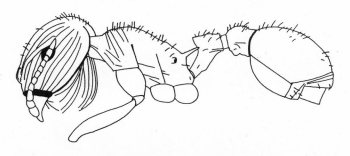

Pogonomyrmex
occidentalis.
*Reddish brown.
The Hawaii
record is
baffling. The
western har-
vester.*

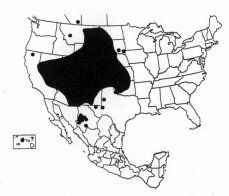

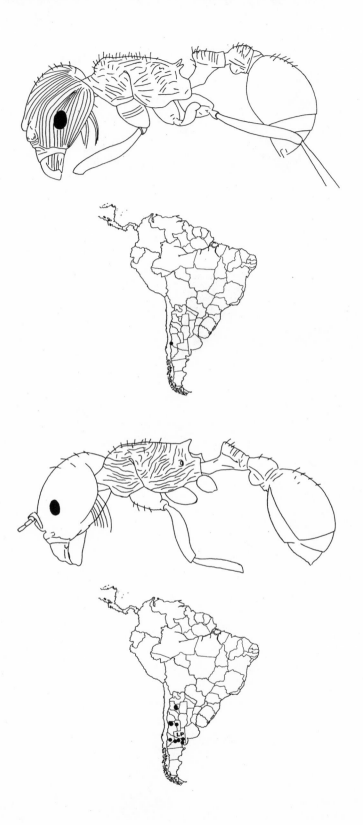

Pogonomyrmex pronotalis. *Black with orange-red gaster. Biology unknown. This is one of the types.*

Pogonomyrmex rastratus. *Variable color. Biology poorly known. The "LP" on the map indicates an unspecified collection locality in the province of La Pampa, Argentina.*

Pogonomyrmex rugosus. *Typically blackish brown, often with a reddish gaster. The rough harvester.*

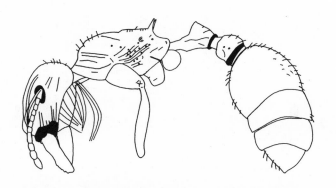

Pogonomyrmex salinus. *Reddish brown. The northernmost of the harvester ants. Also called the owyhee harvester.*

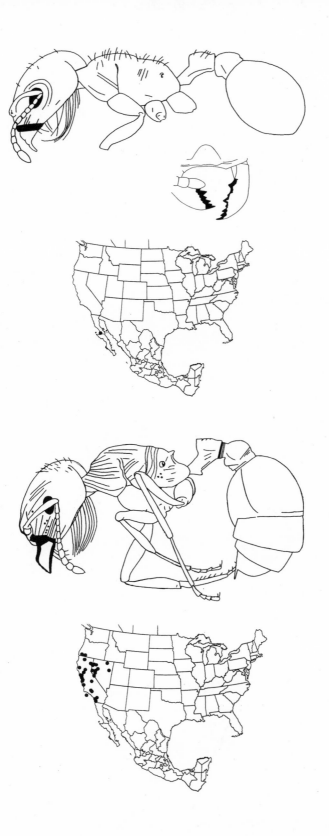

Pogonomyrmex snellingi. *Reddish brown. A new species. The jaws resemble those of the closest relative of the harvesters,* Hylomyrma. *This is a type specimen.* Snelling's harvester.

Pogonomyrmex subdentatus. *Small, reddish brown, and primitive in appearance.*

Pogonomyrmex
subnitidus.
*Reddish brown.
The "?" on the
map indicates
an unspecified
California
collection local-
ity. The "BCN"
indicates an
unspecified
record from
Northern Baja
California.*

Pogonomyrmex
tenuispina.
*Reddish brown.
Biology poorly
known.*

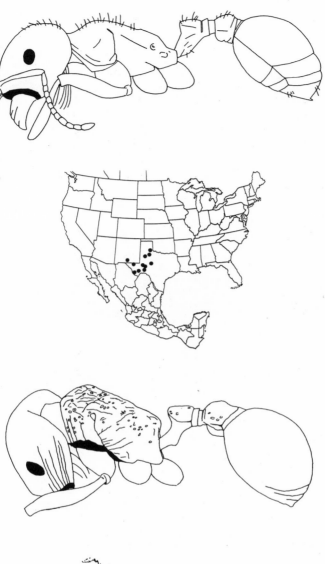

Pogonomyrmex texanus. *Orange-red. Biology poorly known. The common name, Texas harvester, might confuse this species with* P. barbatus, *often called by that name.*

Pogonomyrmex theresiae. *Small, orange and red, intriguing distribution. Biology unknown. Living specimens haven't been reported for one hundred years. Princess Therese's harvester.*

Pogonomyrmex
uruguayensis. *A
small red ant.
The Uruguay
harvester.*

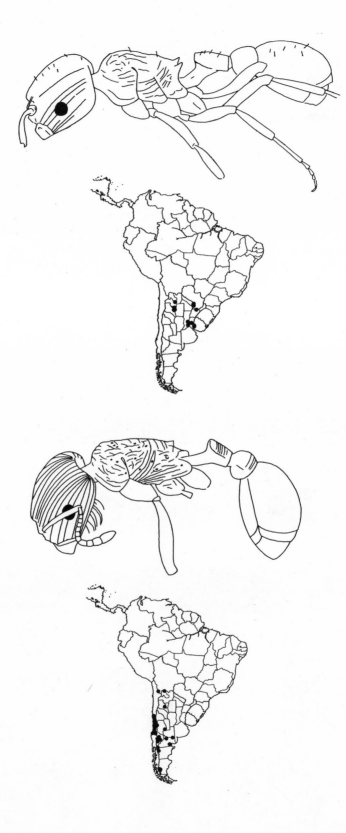

Pogonomyrmex
vermiculatus.
*Variable color.
A synonym
is* variabilis.

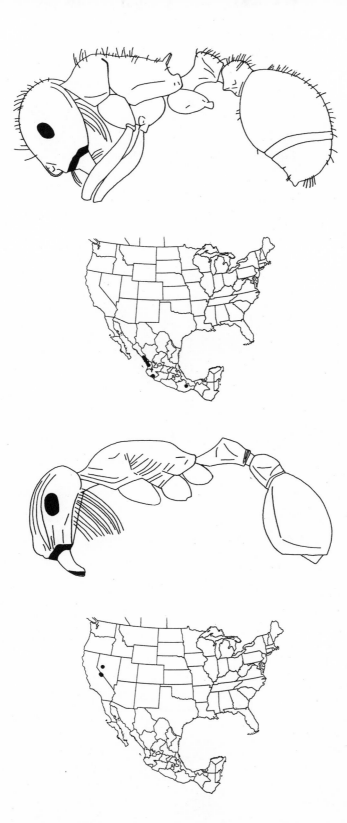

Pogonomyrmex
wheeleri. *Red-*
dish brown.
The largest
North Ameri-
can harvester.
The "?" on the
map indicates
an unspecified
collection local-
ity in the state
of Jalisco,
Mexico.
Wheeler's har-
vester.

Pogonomyrmex
species B. A
new species yet
to be described.
Small and
yellowish red.

Hylomyrma reitteri. *Small, reddish brown ant, closely related to the harvesters. Biology unknown. Used here only as an aid in the study of harvester evolution.*

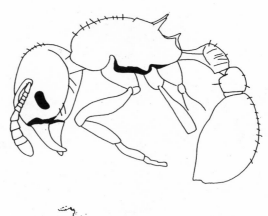

Chapter 7

Harvesters and Humans: Harm or Harmony?

Baxco, Bim, Bif, Bindarine,
Calso, CopRote, Calogreen,
Flea-Not, Fly-Foil, F. & I.,
That's the stuff will make 'em die
— FROM *THE BUG-CATCHERS' CHORUS*

Only six of the harvester ants have pest status. All of them are North American *Pogonomyrmex*. These are the Florida (McCoy and Kaiser 1990), California (Herms 1950), western (Schmutz et al. 1992), red (Nichol 1931), Maricopa (Borth 1986), and owyhee harvester *(P. salinus)* (Fitzner et al. 1979). Benefits have been reported from only four of these and are few in number and small in magnitude. Still, the overall impact of harvesters on humans is difficult to determine because we really don't know what would happen if they were removed from their ecosystems.

The biggest pests are clearly the western and the red, and the first report of pestilential activity came in 1884 when the red harvester was branded a problem for Central Texas gardeners (Nehrling 1884). It didn't seem to bother farmers too much at that time. However, subsequent reports are not so favorable. Yield losses are now on record from seed collection, defoliation, and removal of young and old plants. Those affected include corn, oats, alfalfa, cotton, guayule (a source of rubber), grapes, pastures, shrubs, and date, citrus, apple, pear, and grapefruit trees (Nichol 1931).

Animals are attacked too. The ants annoy livestock and sting horses working in fields, as well as domesticated birds, people, and dairy cows, which are stung on their udders. Grassland erosion is caused by the nest clearings, which remove up to 20 percent of the vegetation in some areas. A nest count in 120 acres of pasture turned up 585 nests (about 5 nests per acre) (Young and Howell 1954).

For at least fifty years the red harvester has been damaging airplane runways and highway surfaces (Zelade 1986). They do this by building their nests at the edge of the tarmac or asphalt, causing potholes and erosion from the outside in. Half of the highway damage in the panhandle region of Texas is caused by this insect, and road crews understandably complain about the painful job. Airborne videography is being used to map red harvester ant infestations in southern Texas (Everitt et al. 1996). The large nest clearings are visible from surveillance airplanes.

The western harvester's damage is done on the range. One assessment discovered 90,000 acres of grazing land denuded of grass by the clearing and feeding activities of *P. occidentalis* (Killough and Hull 1951). Clearings exist at densities of 50 per acre, and erosion is a danger when 20 percent of a grazing area is stripped of plant life by thousands of tiny jaws. Crop seeds are gathered up, as are experimental seeds and seedlings, with one estimate placing this at 2 percent of the available seeds (Rogers 1974). It is unclear how seriously to take the claim that western harvesters compete with pronghorns for grasses. The huge mounds obstruct mowing and harvesting, and their presence along highways causes erosion of the asphalt.

All of the above has earned for the western harvester the title of "most economically important ant pest in Utah" (Knowlton 1953). Only grasshoppers are said to have a more consistent impact on rangelands. However, there are dissenting voices. Infestations might be a *result* of poor ranges, not a cause of their deterioration, and the harmful effects of the ant might be overrated (Wight and Nichols 1966). One report concluded that long-term control might be impossible in any event (Rogers 1987).

The owyhee harvester has effects similar to those of the western. They clear up to 17 percent of infested rangeland (Willard 1964), are occasional nuisances in the basements of houses (Clark 1977), and disturb radioactive waste that has been stored underground (Fitzner et al. 1979). Unlike many ants, harvesters are almost never found in houses. The report for the owyhee species is the only one on record. The Florida, California, and Maricopa harvesters are lawn pests. The last-named ant is also a pest of wheat (Borth, Tickes, and Johnson 1982). The California species kills pigs that spend too much time on the mound (Herms 1950).

There have been many attempts to control harvester ants with chemicals, but field infestations seem to be better controlled with regular cultivation. The first report in 1884 listed poison (an unspecified type), fire, and excavation as unsuccessful against the red harvester. Ranchers have drenched mounds with motor oil and cow dung, with questionable results (Lavigne 1966). The ants can detect some extermination attempts before it's too late. When sunflower seeds were poisoned with arsenic and offered to them, they collected the seeds and stored them in the nest. The next day the seeds were all on the surface again, on the trash heap (Nichol 1931). When benzene hexachloride was used, the ants did not move it away. They moved their nest entrance instead (Warnhoff 1947).

The western harvester provides a few small benefits. For example, Native Americans used it as a living insecticide. They rid their blankets of lice by spreading the fabric out on the mounds (McCook 1882). Today, mounds are checked by mineral prospectors on both continents for microfossils, uranium, manganese, copper, silver, and gold (Hutchins 1966). Farmers feed the gravel to chickens so that their gizzards will have something to grind food with (Lavigne 1966). When I was young and living in College Station, Texas, I placed dead animals on the red harvester mounds and waited until the picked-clean skeletons were ready for display.

The red harvester preys upon termites, crop pests, screwworms, and cattle ear ticks (Parish 1949). The western harvester also preys upon a number of insect pests, such as termites and grubs. The list of benefits is roughly the same for the Florida and owyhee harvesters. The Comanche harvester collects large numbers of fire ant queens following the fire ant's mating flights. Large nests modify the surrounding soil by aerating it via the system of tunnels, an alteration that also increases water penetration (Hunter 1912).

Nitrogen and potassium are concentrated in the soil by the remains of thousands of stored seeds and insects (Mandel and Sorenson 1982).

Insecticides and their effects on the environment are such controversial topics that a short history of their use against harvesters is appropriate here. The following list includes each insecticide, the time it was first used against the ants, and an asterisk for those chemicals that are now superseded. *The Pesticide Manual* (Worthing and Hance 1991) defines superseded insecticides as those that now have "little commercial interest." Some aren't competitive enough against new agents, and some are illegal in areas. Not all of the chemicals used against harvesters were in the manual, which was especially clear about the great and immediate danger to humans from cyanides and methyl bromide.

The first chemical used against harvesters was carbon bisulphide reported by E. A. Popenoe (1904). This was followed by arsenic and London purple (1930s), Velsicol 1068, hexachlorocyclohexane, piperonyl butoxide, piperonyl cyclohexane, benzene hexachloride, sodium cyanide, calcium cyanide (1940s), DDT, chlordane, aldrin, dieldrin, heptachlor, toxaphene, methyl bromide (1950s), Mirex, Kepone, J & J Multipurpose Insect Bait (1960s), Orthene (1970s), and hydramethylnon (also known as Amdro, Combat, and Maxforce) (1980s).

Hydramethylnon (a fluorinated hydrocarbon) under its several trade names and Orthene (an organophosphorus compound) are recommended by current insect control manuals. Orthene is a systemic insecticide that acts like certain nerve gases in the human arsenal. The ants tremble when poisoned with Amdro, and flies were quick to show up at some experimentally treated nests of the Maricopa harvester (Borth, Tickes, and Johnson 1982). Trembling behavior has also been reported in lab colonies where there was no poisoning going on (Wilson 1971). Its significance is unclear. Red harvester workers carry their poisoned dead up to 100 feet from the nest in a manner that suggests a group of pall-bearers. Dead ants are sometimes licked and carried about before they are put out with the trash (Wilson, Durlach, and Roth 1958).

Insects inspire the whole spectrum of sentiments. Anthony Standen, pest controller and author of *Insect Invaders* (1943), was clear about his own feelings: "I hate insects, and my sole interest in them is to be able to destroy them." The other extreme is expressed by Bert Hölldobler and E. O. Wilson in the opening line to their popular work, *Journey to the Ants* (1994): "Our passion is ants. . . ." In all fairness, it seems that lovers of insects know more about them than haters. Most of us, including myself, occupy an intermediate ground between the lovers and haters. What I have for the harvester ants is best described as a healthy curiosity.

Appendix 1

Harvester Ant Names and Their Meanings

The following explanations refer to both scientific and common names. A scientific species name is latinized and consists of two words: the genus and the "specific epithet." In the old days, authors of new species rarely explained the meaning of the name they chose for the previously unknown ant. Why they didn't is a mystery. They might have assumed that their readers would be familiar enough with Latin or Greek to discern the meanings. With this legacy of confusion, I had to make educated guesses most of the time. The Entomological Society of America (ESA) gives its blessing to certain common names (Stoetzel 1989), but there are really no rules to follow. These approved names are listed, as are some less official ones that I pulled from the literature. The common names that I coined for convenience in the text are not listed here.

Harvester Ant Genus EPHEBOMYRMEX ("Youthful Ant")

Ephebomyrmex abdominalis; the waist region of the abdomen is very large.

Ephebomyrmex angustus; part of the ant is narrow, perhaps referring to the head.

Ephebomyrmex brevibarbis; the beard is very short.

Ephebomyrmex cunicularius; it digs in the earth.

Ephebomyrmex fossilis; it is known only from fossils that are thirty million years old.

Ephebomyrmex imberbiculus; it has no beard.

Ephebomyrmex laevigatus; much of the body is smooth.

Ephebomyrmex laevinodis; the top part of the waist is smooth.

Ephebomyrmex mayri; named for Gustav Mayr, who coined the name *Pogonomyrmex* in 1868.

Ephebomyrmex naegelii; named for Naegeli, who collected the specimens.

Ephebomyrmex odoratus; the name suggests that the ant has an aroma, but no explanation was given.

Ephebomyrmex pima; named for the Pima Indian tribe.

Ephebomyrmex saucius; referring either to those who plow the ground or to those who are wounded. Perhaps it refers to the saucer-shaped petiolar node.

Ephebomyrmex schmitti; named for Schmitt, its collector.

Ephebomyrmex sylvestris; one who dwells in the forest.

Ephebomyrmex tenuipubens; this ant has very fine hairs on its body.

Harvester Ant Genus POGONOMYRMEX ("Bearded Ant")

Pogonomyrmex anergismus; lacking a worker class (social parasite).

Pogonomyrmex anzensis; discovered in Anza Desert State Park, California.

Pogonomyrmex apache; named for the Apache Indian tribe.

Pogonomyrmex atratus; a black ant.

Pogonomyrmex badius; not "bad," but reddish brown. Florida harvester ant (ESA name). Also known as the southern harvester ant.

Pogonomyrmex barbatus; with a beard. Red harvester ant (ESA name). Also known as the stinging ant, mound-making ant, agricultural ant, Rostameise (rust-red ant), Ernte-Ameise (harvester ant), hillock ant, hormiga brava (ferocious ant), Bartameise (bearded ant), Säerin (sowing ant), weeding ant, Mexican harvester ant, Texas harvester ant, hormiga colorada (red ant), wóˑlážin coh (Navaho name, large black ant), wóláčížin (Navaho name, red ant), large brown desert ant, and of course, (like many others) red ant. In 1995 the red harvester was nominated as the official state insect of Texas. I was asked for my opinion on this but I explained that the adoption of official bugs was not the function of government. I received no more calls on the subject.

Pogonomyrmex bicolor; two colors are present, red and black.

Pogonomyrmex bigbendensis; discovered in Big Bend National Park, Texas. This name was actually criticized in the literature by an ant biologist. I like it just fine.

Pogonomyrmex bispinosus; it has two spines on its back.

Pogonomyrmex brevispinosus; the spines are short and stubby.

Pogonomyrmex bruchi; named for the entomologist Carlos Bruch.

Pogonomyrmex californicus; named for the state of its capture. California harvester ant (ESA name).

Pogonomyrmex carbonarius; like *atratus,* a black ant.

Pogonomyrmex catanlilensis; discovered near Catanlil, Argentina.

Pogonomyrmex coarctatus; something about this ant is presumably narrow, but I have no idea what that is.

Pogonomyrmex colei; named for Arthur Cole, who wrote the book on *Pogonomyrmex* in 1968, on the hundredth anniversary of the genus.

Pogonomyrmex comanche; named for the Comanche Indian tribe.

Pogonomyrmex desertorum; found in the desert. The desert harvester ant. The Yuma Indian name for *desertorum* is supposedly "Sikupas," but more likely this name was applied to the red, rough, or western harvester.

Pogonomyrmex guatemaltecus; discovered in Guatemala.

Pogonomyrmex huachucanus; discovered in the Huachuca Mountains, Arizona.

Pogonomyrmex inermis; unarmed, lacking defensive spines on its back.

Pogonomyrmex laticeps; something must be hidden, perhaps the tiny flanges at the origin of the waist segments.

Pogonomyrmex lobatus; it has big lobes below its antennae.

Pogonomyrmex longibarbis; the hairs of its beard are long.

Pogonomyrmex magnacanthus; the corners of its eyes are large.

Pogonomyrmex marcusi; named for Harry Marcus, who collected specimens and studied its natural history.

Pogonomyrmex maricopa; named for the Maricopa Indians or Maricopa County, Arizona. Maricopa harvester ant (ESA name).

Pogonomyrmex meridionalis; a southern ant.

Pogonomyrmex micans; a shiny ant.

Pogonomyrmex montanus; it lives in the mountains.

Pogonomyrmex occidentalis; the harvester of the west. Western harvester ant (ESA name). Also known as the occident ant, westliche ant, mound-building prairie ant, a'ni gwi tchuk or a'rran gotsabi (Goshute Indian names, red ant), Dachdeckerin (roofer), Pflasterin (paver) ant, mound-building ant, wóláčí (Navaho name, red ant), wóláčí˙' na˙ t'agí (Navaho name, flying red ant), red harvester.

Pogonomyrmex pronotalis; something about its pronotum.

Pogonomyrmex rastratus; it has a tooth somewhere, presumably the large wedge at the origin of the waist segments.

Pogonomyrmex rugosus; this "rough" ant has wrinkles on its face and back, although it might just as well have been named for its treatment of collectors. Rough harvester ant (ESA name). Also known as the black harvester ant.

Pogonomyrmex salinus; discovered at Soda Springs, California (saline area). This species name has priority over the synonym *P. owyheei,* hence the occasional reference to the "owyhee" harvester ant.

Pogonomyrmex snellingi; named for Roy Snelling, who discovered it. Described in appendix 4.

Pogonomyrmex subdentatus; there is a tooth on the underside of its waist.

Pogonomyrmex subnitidus; not explained by the author, nor do I have an educated guess for the meaning.

Pogonomyrmex tenuispina; the spines on its back are thin.

Pogonomyrmex texanus; discovered in Texas.

Pogonomyrmex theresiae; named for the Bavarian Princess Therese.

Pogonomyrmex uruguayensis; discovered in Uruguay.

Pogonomyrmex vermiculatus; it has a checkerboard pattern on its exoskeleton.

Pogonomyrmex wheeleri; named for William Morton Wheeler, perhaps the most prolific myrmecologist ever.

Pogonomyrmex Species B; this species has not received a formal name because it is known from so little material.

Appendix 2

Identifying Harvester Ants

There are sixty living species of harvester ants of the genera *Pogonomyrmex* and *Ephebomyrmex*. All of these are confined to the New World (North America, South America, Central America, and the Caribbean). Some readers will have no need or desire to identify an insect to species, but for others this might be very important. There are formal, technical ways to identify a harvester ant, and I have provided the means to do so in the keys that follow. However, this process can be tedious if one is not familiar with the terminology and the microscopic anatomy of ants. I have attempted to provide relief with a strategy based largely upon characteristics that do not require a powerful hand lens or microscope. Figure A2.1 illustrates the anatomy of a harvester ant.

The relevant attributes for identification are:

1. collection locality
2. appearance of the ant as seen with a hand lens of 10–20x
3. nest structure
4. nest population
5. behavior
6. color
7. size

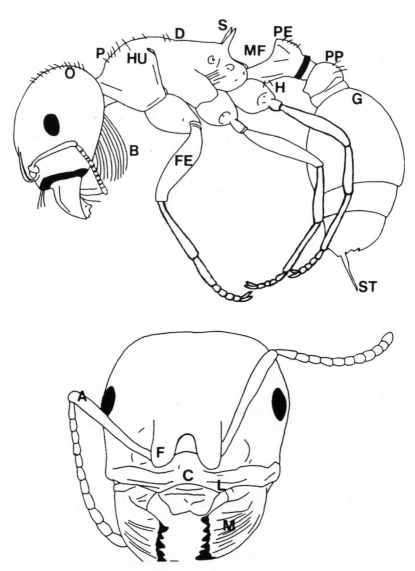

A2.1 Harvester ant anatomy. Top: worker, lateral view. Bottom: worker, frontal view of head.

A: antenna or feeler; the long first segment is called the scape.

B: beard, or psammophore; this is packed with soil and used as a shovel or pail during excavations. Pogonomyrmex means "bearded ant."

C: clypeus; a region in front of the scapes and bordering what appears to be the mouth

D: mesopropodeal depression

F: frontal lobe; a plate that covers the attachment of the antenna to the surface of the head

FE: femur of the foreleg

G: *first or basal segment of the gaster. The gaster is the bulbous region that follows the waspish waist.*

H: *hairs or setae of the* barbatus *species group, on the ventral surface of the petiole. They arise in a region that is developed as a lobe in some species, such as* barbatus *itself, the model used here.*

HU: *humeral region or shoulder*

L: *lateral lobe (or projection) of the clypeus*

M: *mandible or jaw*

MF: *metasternal flange*

O: *occiput or occipital region*

P: *pronotum of thorax*

PE: *petiole; the first segment of the waspish waist. The node is the bulge just beneath the letters PE. The forward stalklike section is called the peduncle.*

PP: *postpetiole; the second and last segment of the waspish waist*

S: *spines of the propodeum. The propodeum is the last part of what appears to be the thorax. The propodeum is actually a part of the abdomen. The alitrunk is the region between but not including the head and the petiole.*

ST: *sting or "stinger"; the famous business end of the harvester ants. The bite is delivered by the jaws and is of no consequence.*

T: *teeth; the "T" is near the apical tooth. The slightly upturned tooth at the base is called the basal tooth and it is contiguous with the basal margin of the mandible.*

Most readers will be collecting in North America. This cuts the problem in half, from sixty to only thirty species. Those who wish to identify the rarely encountered Caribbean or South American species are likely to be specialists, and they should look at the distribution maps, habitus (appearance) illustrations, and the keys.

Given the problem of picking out one species from the thirty that occur in North America, the user should start with the distribution maps. Some species will not occur at the collection locality. The next step is to consult the habitus drawings for all species that do occur at that locality. These provide a lateral view of important features and might be sufficient in and of themselves. Comparisons of nest structure, nest population, behavior, color, and size are provided in table A2.1, which follows. It will often be possible to identify a specimen without using the keys below.

A note about preservation: Preserving ant specimens is simple. The simplest and perhaps best way to preserve them is to place them in 70 percent ordinary rubbing alcohol. The traditional method is to preserve them dry by gluing them to a small piece of paper or card and running the insect pin through the card (fig. A2.2). It is best to glue the specimens on the side using household glue, so that the undersurface is not obscured. The problem with the traditional method is that other insects can eat the specimens (fig. A2.3).

Now for an example of identification. You collected an ant that you believe to be a harvester and you want to know which

A2.2 Looking down on an ant from the famous Harvard collection. The specimen has been "carded" (glued to paper). This is Pogonomyrmex atratus *from Argentina.*

A2.3 This used to be an intact winged harvester ant. A carpet beetle reduced it to a worthless husk.

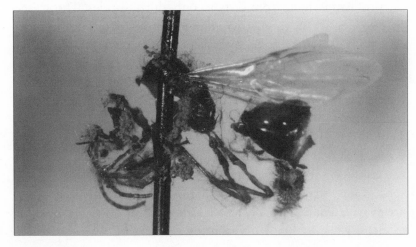

species it is (if you remain unsure even of the ant's status as a harvester, flip through the illustrations or see Bolton 1994 or Hölldobler and Wilson 1990). The nest is in your backyard in central Texas. Using the distribution maps for North American species, you reduce the possibilities to just four: *E. imberbiculus, P. apache, P. barbatus,* and *P. comanche.* Now you look at the four habitus illustrations that accompany each map. Sometimes there is a real sore thumb in a group; in this case it is *Ephebomyrmex imberbiculus,* which looks nothing like your specimen or any of the other three. You verify this elimination by looking up the attributes of that species in table A2.1. *E. imberbiculus* is eliminated, so it must be one of the other three. The nest structure is a large mound (several feet across) and is sprinkled liberally with gravel and perhaps other such oddities as colorful chips of broken glass. Of the three candidates, only the red harvester ant *(Pogonomyrmex barbatus)* seems to satisfy this criterion. You also note that there is a seemingly endless stream of large red ants racing to and from the central entrance(s) in the late morning. They run directly at you in scattered hordes, climb up your trousers, and try to sting your hands and feet viciously wherever and whenever possible. According to nest population, behavior, color, and size you corroborate your identification: *Pogonomyrmex barbatus* (with the officially approved common name of red harvester ant).

TABLE A2.1.

HARVESTER ANT CHARACTERISTICS

FOR SPECIES IDENTIFICATION

	Nest Structure	Nest Population	Behavior	Color	Size
Species with Ventral Surface Hairs[a]					
P. barbatus	M	P	A	R	L
P. rugosus	M	P	A	B, B+R, (R)	L
P. desertorum	C	F	D	R	S
P. apache	C, (M)	F	D	R	L
P. bicolor*	M	P	D	B+R, (R)	L
P. texanus*	C	F	D	O, (R)	L
P. bigbendensis**	C	?	?	R	S
P. tenuispina**	C	P	?	R	L
P. wheeleri**	M	P	A	R	L

	Nest Structure	Nest Population	Behavior	Color	Size
*P. anergismus***	social parasites with no worker class and no nest of their own				
*P. colei***	social parasites with no worker class and no nest of their own				

Species Lacking Ventral Surface Hairs and Lacking Eye Whorls or Loops[b]

	Nest Structure	Nest Population	Behavior	Color	Size
P. badius	the only harvester found east of the Mississippi and confined to that area as well				
P. occidentalis	M	P	A	R	L
P. salinus	M	P	A, (D)	R	L, S
P. subnitidus	C	P	A	R	L
P. subdentatus	C	F	D	R	L, S
*P. brevispinosus**	C	F	D	R	S
*P. montanus***	C	P	A	R	L

Species with Well-Defined Eye Loops[c]

	Nest Structure	Nest Population	Behavior	Color	Size
P. californicus	C, M	P	A	R	L, S
P. maricopa	C, M	P	A	R	L
*P. magnacanthus**	C	F	D	R	S
*P. comanche**	C	F, P	D	R	L
*P. anzensis***	C	?	?	R	L, S
*P. snellingi***	?	?	?	R	L
*P. sp. B***	?	?	?	?	S

Small and Obscure Species[d]

	Nest Structure	Nest Population	Behavior	Color	Size
*E. imberbiculus**	C	F	D	R	S
*P. huachucanus***	C	F	A, D	R	S
*E. pima***	C	F	D	R	S
*E. laevinodis***	C	?	?	R	S
*P. guatemaltecus***	C	?	?	R	S

Note: This table is split into groups that share characters that might require microscopic observation. Mound and colony descriptions refer to mature colonies. The species within these groups are listed in an order that roughly reflects the likelihood of collection (descending order). Parentheses enclose a less common or an uncommon condition. When the tips above result in a tie between candidates for identification, see the keys that follow for additional characteristics.

* = not as commonly collected as species without asterisks

** = unlikely to be collected

A = aggressive (will charge and sting readily and painfully)

B = brownish to blackish

B+R = red and brownish black in a single individual

C = cryptic (easily overlooked) mound or small, fairly obscure mound. These nests can be marked by little more than a small nest entrance.

D = docile (runs away and/or hides, becomes immobile, does not sting readily)

F = few (a dozen or so to just a few hundred worker ants)

L = large (usually 6 millimeters or longer)

M = large mound or cleared area (can be many feet in diameter). Often visible at quite a distance. Such mounds are often covered with pebbles.

O = orange-red

P = populous (can be many hundreds or thousands of worker ants)

R = red

S = small (usually less than 6 millimeters)

? = unknown

[a]All of these species have one or a few tiny hairs on the ventral surface of the first segment of the waist. No other species do. See the drawing of *P. barbatus* for an example of this condition.

[b]These seven species lack the tiny hairs of the *P. barbatus* group and they lack a series of complete loops that surround the eye. These loops are raised ridges of the exoskeleton and must be viewed with magnification. Specimens of *P. salinus*, *P. subnitidus*, and *P. montanus* sometimes have weak or broken loops and might be confused with the seven species of the next set, which have a series of well-defined, unbroken loops about each eye. See the drawing of *P. maricopa* for an indication of these loops.

[c]These seven species have a series of well-defined loops that surround each eye. Magnification is required to determine the presence of the loops.

[d]These five species are quite small and are unlikely to be collected.

Keys to the Identification of All Harvesters

These keys provide the formal means to identify all of the *Pogonomyrmex* and *Ephebomyrmex* harvester ants. Those unfamiliar with the terminology should refer to the explanations of figure A2.1, the individual species drawings, and the glossary. The keys are standard dichotomous keys used by biologists to identify species. The numbers represent couplets, while the letters represent lugs (e.g., key I, couplet 6, lug b, refers to "head and alitrunk black or blackish"). The number at the end of a lug tells the reader which couplet to go to next (in the above example, if the condition is satisfied the reader would refer to couplet 7), unless the identification has been made, in which case the species is named. The lug the reader moves to depends upon the characteristics of the specimen. The phrase "in part" is used in the keys when dealing with a species that is so variable it cannot appear in only one place; it appears two or more times in the keys.

The keys assume that the ant has been identified to subfamily Myrmicinae and that the specimens are of the worker caste (with two necessary exceptions, described below). Complete keys to gynes and males cannot be comprehensive at this time because one or both of the reproductive castes of many species are unknown. For keys to South American gynes and males see Gallardo (1932) and Kusnezov (1978). For North American species, see Cole (1968) and Snelling (1981). For preliminary identification of the ant to subfamily, see Hölldobler and Wilson (1990) and/or Bolton (1994). The anatomy of a typical harvester ant is illustrated in figure A2.1. For a book on ants written by experts and accessible to all, see Hölldobler and Wilson (1994). The work of Shattuck (1987) was a great aid in the separation of the species that comprise the "*occidentalis* complex" of Cole (1968).

Ephebomyrmex and *Pogonomyrmex* are members of the tribe Myrmicini. This tribe is recognized by the pectinate (comblike) tibial spurs of the middle and/or hind legs. These are not visible by casual inspection. They require a microscope. Among the North and South American members of the tribe, *Pogonomyrmex* species are distinguished by a clear synapomorphy (shared, derived character), the psammophore, or well-developed beard.

Ephebomyrmex presents a more difficult problem. Although there is probably complete agreement about the monophyly of *Ephebomyrmex* plus *Pogonomyrmex*, I know of no single character that can be used to separate *Ephebomyrmex* from *Hylomyrma*, *Manica*, and North American *Myrmica* (other members of tribe Myrmicini). However, *Ephebomyrmex* workers can be distinguished from *Pogonomyrmex* workers by two primitive characters: their poorly developed beard and their relatively swollen clypeal plate (figs. A2.4–A2.7). North American (mainland) *Ephebomyrmex* can be identified by the following characters: (1) lack of psammophore (but sparse setae often present), (2) dentary margin of mandible roughly transverse, (3) alitrunk profile almost continuous and roughly convex (not broken by a conspicuous mesopropodeal de-

A2.4 *The lower surface of this* Ephebomyrmex *harvester shows a few sparse setae but no beard. For the* Pogonomyrmex *beard, see figure 1.6.*

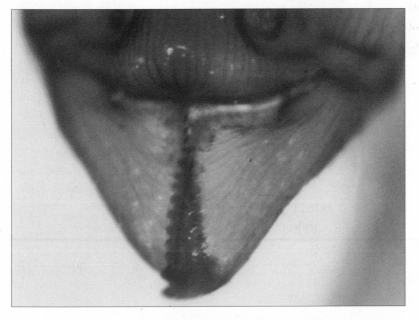

A2.5 *This head-on view of the clypeus of a relative of the harvester ants shows the bulging area characteristic of* Ephebomyrmex, *but in an extreme form. This part of the clypeus is the central region just above the jaws.*

A2.6 *The bulging clypeus of* Ephebomyrmex.

A2.7 *The flattened clypeus of* Pogonomyrmex.

pression), (4) cephalic sculpture coarsely rugo-reticulate, (5) small size (app. 4–6 mm in length), and (6) docile behavior.

There are only three such species known at the present time, so the specimen can be easily compared to the line drawings of *E. imberbiculus*, *E. laevinodis*, and *E. pima*. If the specimen is from Haiti, has been identified to this tribe, and has no psammophore, it is probably *Ephebomyrmex saucius* or *schmitti* (check against line drawings). If beardless and from South America, has been identified to this tribe, and the dentary margin of the mandible is roughly transverse (as opposed to the oblique margin of *Hylomyrma*), and/or the anterior margin of the clypeus is convex, then it is *Ephebomyrmex*. Most *Ephebomyrmex* are South American, but it is not difficult to compare the specimen with the drawings provided herein. In all cases, it is wise to use the keys and the distribution maps. Neither *Ephebomyrmex* nor *Pogonomyrmex* are transported by commerce and, in regard to range expansion, they are not a particularly vagile group (surprising in the case of *Pogonomyrmex*). For example, *P. badius* has been known for almost two hundred years, but there are no records west of the Mississippi River, even though the ant is found from the eastern bank to the Atlantic Ocean. The river remains an efficient barrier to the westward range expansion of this large insect. As a result, distribution maps can be quite useful in identification.

Two of the sixty species are inquilines (social parasites in nests of congeners), and they have no worker caste. Both are *Pogonomyrmex,* but the general collector is unlikely to encounter them. They have a seta or setae on the venter of the peduncle of the petiole (as do all other members of the *P. barbatus* species complex). The gynes have a distinct median impression on the dorsum of the petiolar node (which is conoid in profile), and the males have either the impression or the conoid profile (Snelling 1981). The gynes have six mandibular teeth and the males have short, coarse setae on the alitrunk, these traits separating them as a duo from the rest of the species complex. The two inquilines can be separated from one another by the basal face of the propodeum, which is vermiculate-rugose in both sexes of *P. colei*. In *P. anergismus,* the basal face is striate or finely rugose, sometimes with a smooth area. *Pogonomyrmex colei* is recorded only from rough harvester nests, whereas *P. anergismus* is known from the nests of the rough and the red harvesters.

Two *Pogonomyrmex* species have a major-worker class (distinguished by large heads), which was not used in the construction of the keys. If major workers of these strongly polymorphic species must be identified, the solution is simple. If the major worker is South American and the propodeum is armed with spines, it is *P. coarctatus*. If the major worker is North American and the propodeum lacks spines, it is *P. badius*.

Keys to the Nonparasitic Species of EPHEBOMYRMEX and POGONOMYRMEX

I. KEY TO *EPHEBOMYRMEX* (ALL SPECIES)

1. a. dorsum of basal segment of gaster with longitudinal rugae or striae 2

   b. dorsum of basal segment of gaster without longitudinal rugae or striae 5

2. a. dorsum of basal segment of gaster entirely or mostly covered by rugae or striations ....
   .... *mayri* (Colombia, Guyana) L = 7.6–9.0 mm

   b. rugae or striae of dorsum of basal segment of gaster confined to basal half of segment, sometimes found only near insertion of postpetiole 3

3. a. anterior margin of clypeus convex, with small median triangular tooth .... *sylvestris* (Venezuela) L = 5.0 mm

   b. anterior margin of clypeus slightly excised or almost straight, but not broadly convex, margin without a small median triangular tooth 4

4. a. petiole and postpetiole not massive (see species drawing) ....
   .... *naegelii* (much of South America) L = 4.0–5.0 mm

   b. petiole and postpetiole massive (see species drawing) .....
   ....
   abdominalis (southern South America) L = 4.0–4.5 mm

5. a. maxillary palps with 5 segments, labial palps with 4 segments 6

   b. maxillary palps with 4 segments, labial palps with 3 segments 8

6. a. head and alitrunk yellow or reddish, but not black ....
   .... *odoratus* (Argentina, Chile) L = 4.4–4.8 mm

   b. head and alitrunk black or blackish 7

7. a. occiput and much of thoracic dorsum smooth, shining, few if any reticulations present, same for dorsum of petiolar node ....
   .... *laevigatus* (Argentina, Chile) L = 4.5–5.0 mm

   b. occiput with prominent reticulations and areolations, same for dorsum of thorax and petiolar node ....
   .... *angustus* (Argentina, Chile) L = 4.6–6.0 mm

8. a. alitrunk in profile with distinct mesopropodeal depression, so that profile is not broadly convex (South America) .. 9

b. alitrunk in profile without distinct mesopropodeal depression, so that profile is broadly convex 10

9. a. head and alitrunk yellow, orange, or red, but not black ..
    .... *cunicularius* (southern South America)
    L = 6.2–9.4 mm (worker), L = 12.0 mm (ergatogyne)

b. head and alitrunk black or blackish red ....
    .... *brevibarbis* (Argentina) L = 5.0–7.0 mm

10. a. anterior margin of clypeus broadly convex, head and alitrunk blackish or blackish red, setae of dorsum of basal segment of gaster erect or semierect and black (Haiti) 11

b. anterior margin of clypeus excised or straight, but not broadly convex, head and alitrunk yellow, red, or reddish brown, but never blackish (not Haiti) 12

11. a. petiolar node in dorsal view fan-shaped or shaped like baseball catcher's mitt (rugae present but rather sparse) .... *saucius* (Haiti) L = 5.0–5.5 mm

b. petiolar node in dorsal view miter-shaped (node covered with coarse rugae) .... *schmitti* (Haiti) L = 3.5–4.5 mm

12. a. lateral clypeal projections prominent 13

b. lateral clypeal projections absent or very weak 14

13. a. propodeal spines absent, dorsum of petiolar node with little or no rugae, the surface almost smooth ....
    .... *laevinodis* (Baja California) L = 3.5 mm

b. propodeal spines present, dorsum of petiolar node with conspicuous rugae ....
    .... *imberbiculus* (U.S., Mexico) L = 4.0–4.8 mm

14. a. dorsum of basal segment of gaster with fine and appressed setae (lying flat or nearly so against the surface), dorsum of segment smooth and shining (not shagreened) ....
    .... *tenuipubens* (Argentina, Paraguay) L = 5.0 mm

b. setae on dorsum of basal segment of gaster erect or suberect (not appressed), dorsum of gaster at least lightly shagreened .... *pima* (U.S., Mexico) L = 3.5–4.0 mm

KEY TO NORTH AMERICAN *POGONOMYRMEX*

1. a. thoracic setae dark (brownish black), propodeum unarmed (lacking spines or tubercles), clypeal apron strongly bidentate ....
    ..... *guatemaltecus* (Guatemala, Mexico) L = 5.0–5.5 mm

    b. thoracic setae clear or whitish 2

2. a. venter of petiolar peduncle (near area that is or would be occupied by the ventral process) with one or more distinct setae (*barbatus* species complex) 3

    b. venter of petiolar peduncle (near area that is or would be occupied by the ventral process) without distinct seta(e) 11

3. a. occipital corners with conspicuous rugae or striae 4

    b. occipital corners without conspicuous rugae or striae (smooth and shining) 7

4. a. rugae of thoracic dorsum with conspicuous reticulation, cephalic and thoracic rugae coarse, widely spaced, head and/or thorax usually blackish or dark brown .... *rugosus* (U.S., Mexico) L = 7.0–9.5 mm

    b. rugae of thoracic dorsum without conspicuous reticulation, color red or brownish red, but not blackish 5

5. a. very large ants (9.5–11.5 mm), red, scape base strongly compressed (almost spatulate) and usually with pubescence, scape shaft with a few rugae or striae .... *wheeleri* (Mexico)

    b. lacking the above character combination 6

6. a. scape base strongly developed (flared) with a trough or concavity, lateral clypeal lobes conspicuous, basal mandibular tooth slightly offset .... *barbatus* (U.S., Mexico) L = 7.0–9.5 mm

    b. scape base only moderately developed, lacking conspicuous trough or concavity, lateral clypeal lobes absent or inconspicuous, basal mandibular tooth not slightly offset, gaster often (but not always) blackish .... *bicolor* (U.S., Mexico) L = 7.2–8.2 mm

7. a. propodeum unarmed (lacking spines or tubercles) 8

    b. propodeum armed (with spines or tubercles) 10

8. a. mandible with less than 7 teeth, basalmost tooth strongly offset from margin, in full-face view cephalic rugae often sparse, base of antenna scape weakly developed, hardly flared .... *bigbendensis* (U.S., Mexico) L = 5.5–6.0 mm

    b. lacking the above character combination 9

9. a. declivious face of propodeum without rugae or striae, color usually orange-yellow, but sometimes deep red, clypeal

margin deeply excised ... *texanus* (U.S.) L = 9.0–10.0 mm

   b. declivious face of propodeum with rugae or striae, color usually red, clypeal margin very strongly excised, sometimes almost to the frontal lobes ....
............................*apache* (U.S., Mexico) L = 7.5–9.0 mm

10. a. lateral clypeal projections prominent, base of antenna scape with conspicuous trough or depression ....
.... *tenuispina* (U.S., Mexico) L = 6.5–8.5 mm

   b. lateral clypeal projections absent or inconspicuous, base of antenna scape without conspicuous trough or depression .... *desertorum* (U.S., Mexico) L = 5.5–6.5 mm

11. a. with head in full-face view, sides of head behind eyes converging posteriorly, propodeum unarmed, with head in lateral view, eye located distinctly below midpoint of side of head ....
.... *badius* (U.S.) L = 7.0–11.0 mm (including major)

   b. lacking the above character combination 12

12. a. mandible with 6 teeth 13

   b. mandible with 7 or more teeth 14

13. a. eye surrounded by whorled rugae (circumocular whorls), propodeum unarmed .... *anzensis* (U.S.) L= 6.0 mm

   b. eye without circumocular whorls, propodeum armed .....
.... *huachucanus* (U.S., Mexico) L = 4.5–5.0 mm

14. a. cephalic interrugal sculpture beaded, dorsum of petiolar node not distinctly flattened 15

   b. cephalic interrugal sculpture not presenting a beaded appearance, or if beaded, then dorsum of petiolar node is distinctly flattened 20

15. a. basal mandibular tooth strongly offset from basal margin ..... *occidentalis* (U.S., Canada, Mexico) L = 6.5–8.5 mm

   b. basal mandibular tooth not strongly offset 16

16. a. eyes with circumocular whorls, dorsum of both petiolar and postpetiolar nodes with few or no rugae, propodeal spines (if present), usually little more than tubercles ....
.... *maricopa* (in part) (U.S., Mexico) L = 6.0–9.0 mm

   b. eyes without circumocular whorls, or if whorls are present, then conspicuous propodeal spines are also present, dorsum of petiolar and postpetiolar nodes usually with at least a few distinct rugae 17

17. a. alitrunk profile rather convex in outline, ventral process of petiole very well developed, ventral process of post-petiole robust .... *subdentatus* (U.S.) L = 6.0 mm

b. lacking the above character combination 18

18. a. frontal lobes large, broadly and evenly convex, scape base very well developed, propodeal spines (if present) short, ventral process of petiolar peduncle absent or weak .... *brevispinosus* (U.S.) L = 5.5–6.0 mm

b. lacking the above character combination 19

19. a. base of antenna scape angular and dorsum of petiolar and postpetiolar nodes with 5 or more rugae on posterior half .... *montanus* (U.S.), length = 6.0–6.5 mm

b. base of antenna scape rounded or angular, if angular then dorsum of petiolar and postpetiolar nodes with less than 5 distinct rugae on posterior half .... *salinus* (U.S., Canada) L = 5.0–7.0 mm

20. a. propodeal spines present 21

b. propodeal spines absent (tubercles at best) 23

21. a. eyes with circumocular whorls, basal face of propodeum in profile not roughly horizontal, but sloping so that ali-trunk is rather broadly convex, basal margin of mandible at least weakly convex (not straight) 22

b. eye usually not surrounded by unbroken circumocular whorls, but if whorls are present then basal margin of man-dible is roughly straight, basal face of propodeum in profile is almost horizontal so that alitrunk profile is not broadly convex, propodeal spines are well developed .... *subnitidus* (U.S., Mexico) L = 7.0 mm

22. a. dorsum of petiolar node (in profile) conspicuously flattened and covered with conspicuous rugae, propodeal spines well developed .... *comanche* (U.S.) L = 6.5–8.0 mm

b. lacking above character combination .... *maricopa* (in part) (U.S., Mexico) L = 6.0–9.0 mm

23. a. dentary margin of mandible not roughly transverse but oblique, basal tooth strongly offset from basal margin, which is short .... *snellingi* (Mexico) L = 6.5 mm

b. lacking above character combination 24

24. a. dorsum of first gaster segment smooth and shiny (lacking shagreen), circumocular whorls few and weak, basal man-

dibular tooth slightly offset from margin, alitrunk in profile without conspicuous mesopropodeal depression, propodeum unarmed .... species B (U.S.) L = 4.0 mm

    b. lacking above character combination 25

25. a. eye very large (eye length roughly equal to distance between eye and mandible insertion), small ants (4.7–5.2 mm) .... *magnacanthus* (U.S., Mexico)

    b. eye not unusually large (eye length clearly less than distance between eye and mandible insertion) 26

26. a. cephalic interrugal areolation absent to moderate (never beaded), interrugal areolation of mesopleuron and pronotal sides very weak to absent, interrugal spaces shiny .... *californicus* (U.S., Mexico) L = 5.5–8.7 mm

    b. cephalic interrugal areolation of head, mesopleuron, and pronotal sides moderate to strong, interrugal spaces subopaque .... *maricopa* (in part) (U.S., Mexico) L = 6.0–9.0 mm

KEY TO SOUTH AMERICAN *POGONOMYRMEX*

1. a. interrugal areolation dense, presenting a beaded appearance 2

    b. interrugal areolation not dense enough to present a beaded appearance 17

2. a. propodeum unarmed (with tubercles at best) 3

    b. propodeum armed with short or long spines 4

3. a. dorsum of first gaster segment partly or entirely covered with conspicuous longitudinal rugae .... *longibarbis* (in part) (Argentina, Bolivia) L = 6.0–7.0 mm

    b. dorsum of first gaster segment without rugae .... *inermis* (Argentina) L = 5.0–6.5 mm

4. a. humeral angles rounded, not sharp 5

    b. humeral angles sharp (not smoothly rounded) 6

5. a. scape base strongly developed, trumpet-shaped .... *bispinosus* (Chile) L = 7.8–8.0 mm

    b. scape base only moderately developed, not flared into trumpet-shape ....*uruguayensis* (Argentina, Uruguay) L = 5.5–6.5 mm

6. a. head, alitrunk, and abdomen all black or blackish (I have heard that red-headed *P. carbonarius* workers exist, but I

have not seen any nor have I encountered them in a published report.) 7

  b. of head, alitrunk, and abdomen, at least one not black or blackish 9

7. a. propodeal spines connected by prominent keel, dorsum of first segment of gaster mostly or entirely covered by conspicuous longitudinal rugae ....
.... *carbonarius* (Argentina) L = 6.5–7.0 mm

  b. propodeal spines lacking a prominent connecting keel 8

8. a. basal margin of mandible roughly straight, not convex, at least one mandible with 7–8 teeth ....
.... *atratus* (Argentina) L = 6.5–7.0 mm

  b. basal margin of mandible at least slightly convex, usually at least one mandible with only 6 teeth ....
vermiculatus (in part) (Argentina, Chile) L = 4.9–7.5 mm

9. a. metasternal flanges absent, weak, or difficult to discern with alitrunk in profile view 10

  b. metasternal flanges at least moderately developed, clearly visible with alitrunk in profile (more typical of the genus) 11

10. a. dorsum of first gaster segment without rugae ....
.... *laticeps* (Argentina) L = 8.0–8.5 mm

  b. dorsum of first gaster segment entirely or mostly covered with longitudinal rugae ....
longibarbis (in part) (Argentina, Bolivia) L = 6.0–7.0 mm

11. a. metasternal flanges very large (reminiscent of some *Ephebomyrmex* species), head and gaster orange, alitrunk black, basal face of propodeum in profile almost horizontal, rugae covering dorsum of first gaster segment ....
.... *rastratus* (Argentina) L = 6.0–7.8 mm

  b. lacking above character combination 12

12. a. antenna scape short, in repose not greatly surpassing posterior corner of eye ....
.... *meridionalis* (Argentina) L = 6.5 mm

  b. antenna scape long, in repose approaching or exceeding midpoint between corner of eye and occiput 13

13. a. head red or reddish 14

  b. head black 15

14. a. ammochaetae of psammophore long ....

longibarbis (in part) (Argentina, Bolivia) L = 6.0–7.0 mm

b. ammochaetae of psammophore short ....
vermiculatus (in part) (Argentina, Chile) L = 4.9–7.5 mm

15. a. in full-face view, conspicuous interrugal reticulation covering most of head, head and alitrunk black, gaster orange or red 16

b. in full-face view, any conspicuous interrugal reticulation · is confined to posterior half of head ....
vermiculatus (in part) (Argentina, Chile) L = 4.9–7.5 mm

16. a. dorsum of first segment of gaster entirely covered by longitudinal rugae ....
.... *catanlilensis* (Argentina) L = 7.0–8.0 mm

b. dorsum of first segment of gaster without rugae ....
.... *pronotalis* (Argentina) L = 7.0 mm

17. a. propodeum lacking spines (tubercles at best), rugae or striae present on dorsum of first gaster segment at insertion of postpetiole, basal margin of mandible roughly straight ..
.... *theresiae* (Ecuador) L = 4.5–5.5 mm

b. propodeum with spines, rugae or striae absent from dorsum of first gaster segment, basal margin of mandible at least slightly convex 18

18. a. scapes long, in repose approaching or exceeding midpoint between corner of eye and occiput ....
.... *lobatus* (Argentina, Brazil, Uruguay) L = 7.5–9.0 mm

b. scapes short, in repose not greatly surpassing posterior corner of eye 19

19. a. metasternal flanges in profile poorly developed, inconspicuous or absent 20

b. metasternal flanges in profile conspicuous, more typical of the genus 21

20. a. scape base with conspicuous depression or trough, femur of foreleg weakly incrassate at best, propodeal spines without connecting keel, worker caste strongly polymorphic with big-headed majors ....
coarctatus (Argentina, Uruguay) L = 7.5–12.0 mm (including major)

b. scape base trough absent or weak, femur of foreleg strongly incrassate, propodeal spines with connecting keel, worker caste weakly polymorphic ....
.... *bruchi* (Argentina) L = 7.2–9.0 mm

21. a. occipital corners with conspicuous rugae or striae, lateral clypeal projections only moderately developed ....
.... *micans* (Argentina, Brazil) L = 6.5–8.0 mm
b. occipital corners without conspicuous rugae or striae, lateral clypeal projections strongly developed ....
.....................................*marcusi* (Bolivia) L = 7.0–9.0 mm

Appendix 3

Characters Used in Phylogeny Reconstruction

A character is a property of an organism that can be used to identify and classify it. For example, one of the characters of the class Mammalia is the presence of milk-producing glands in the female.

The character, or data, tables (tables A3.1 and A3.2) contain all the characters used to identify and classify the harvester ants (given in the list that follows). The tables hold ninety-seven columns, with each column corresponding to each of the ninety-seven characters. For example, character number 1 in the list is the width of the head. If a species (in this case the worker) has a narrow head, it receives a "0" in the data table at the first position (the position for character 1) on that species' row. If it has a broad head, it receives a "1." The red harvester, *Pogonomyrmex barbatus,* has a broad head, so it receives a 1 (table A3.1). At the far end of its row of ninety-seven characters, at position ninety-seven, the red harvester receives a 0 because it mates on the ground (character 97). The characters have not actually been labeled by their numbers in the tables because the tables would expand to an awkward size, but it is not difficult to count across a row from left to right.

A computer analysis requires numerical codes of this kind to do its work of finding the best evolutionary tree given the characters at hand. The best tree in this regard is the shortest one that is consistent with the data (see *mapping characters* and *character-optimization procedure* in the glossary for related ideas). The shortest tree is considered the best answer simply because, in science, simple answers are favored over complex ones. This is called the "principle of parsimony." The length of a tree is measured in terms of the total number of character changes (e.g., the change from not having a beard to having a beard) required by the data used to build it. The fewer the number of character changes, the shorter the tree and the simpler the answer. If further changes are made, the length of the tree as calculated by the computer usually changes, too. Sometimes there are two or more equally valid answers, and something like an average value of many trees is reported. That is what has happened with the analysis of the characters of the harvester ants as we know those characters today. More data and different methods might give a different result.

Both the data and the methods can be checked and even worked out by hand by anyone who cares to do so. Evolutionary work has come a long way since authorities simply wrote down their version of the tree of life for the rest of us to accept.

I. Worker Caste

A. CEPHALIC CHARACTERS
1. Dimensions of head capsule (in full-face view):
   width not exceeding length (0); width exceeding length (1)
2. Shape of head capsule (in full-face view):
   sides of head behind eyes not converging strongly toward occipital corners (0); sides of head behind eyes converging strongly toward occipital corners (i.e., head narrowing) (1)
3. Cephalic rugae (divergence, in full-face view):
   rugae diverging toward occipital corners (0); rugae not diverging toward occipital corners (i.e., rugae are roughly parallel) (1)
4. Cephalic rugae (coarseness):
   rugae coarse (0); rugae fine (1)
5. Cephalic rugae (density):
   rugae widely spaced (0); rugae closely spaced (dense) (1)

6. Cephalic rugae (circumocular whorls):
   whorls absent (o); whorls incomplete or occasional (1); whorls present and complete (2)

7. Cephalic rugae (occipital corners):
   rugae present (o); rugae absent, weak striae present at best (1)

8. Cephalic rugae (conspicuous reticulation, in full-face view):
   reticulation absent (o); reticulation covering part but not most of head (1); reticulation covering most or all of head (2)

9. Cephalic areolation ("punctation," in full-face view):
   ordered in decreasing density: (o); (1); (2); (3)

10. Eye (position, in full-face view):
   eye anterior to the midpoint of the side of the head (o); eye centered, or slightly posterior to the midpoint of the side of the head (1)

11. Eye (shape, in full-face view):
   eye convex, protruding from the side of the head (o); eye flattened, not protruding from the side of the head (1)

12. Frontal lobe (shape):
   contour angular or roughly straight (o); contour convex or rounded (1)

13. Frontal depression (depth):
   deep (walls steep) (o); shallow (walls not steep) (1)

14. Lateral clypeal projections (development):
   prominent (o); moderately developed (1); absent or inconspicuous (2)

15. Clypeus (anterior margin):
   convex (o); roughly straight (1); moderately excised (2); deeply excised (3)

16. Clypeus (anterior margin):
   bidentate (o); not bidentate (1)

17. Clypeus (anterior margin):
   median triangular tooth absent (o); median triangular tooth present (1)

18. Clypeus (surface contour):
   surface raised, appearing to bulge (o); surface flattened, not appearing to bulge (1)

19. Antenna (scape length, in repose):
   scape approaching or surpassing the midpoint between the posterior edge of the eye and the occipital margin (long) (o);

scape not greatly surpassing the posterior edge of the eye (short) (1)

20. Antenna (scape thickness):
thick (0); thin or slender (1)

21. Antenna (scape rugosity):
rugae extensive (0); rugae moderate to weak (1); rugae absent (2)

22. Antenna (scape base, curvature):
scape bent or strongly curved near base (0); scape straight or smoothly curved near base (1)

23. Antenna (scape base, development):
weakly developed, hardly exceeding width of contiguous shaft (0); moderately developed but not trumpet-shaped or massive (1); strongly developed, trumpet-shaped or massive (2)

24. Antenna (scape base, depression or trough):
depression absent or very weak (0); depression distinct but not deep (1); depression deep (2)

25. Mandible (number of teeth):
less than 7 (5–6) (0); 7 (rarely 8) (1)

26. Mandible (tooth configuration):
basal tooth not offset from basal margin of mandible (0); basal tooth offset from basal margin of mandible (1)

27. Mandible (tooth development):
counting from apical tooth, no. 4 conspicuously smaller than no. 3 (0); counting from apical tooth, no. 4 about as long as no. 3 (1)

28. Mandible (contour of basal margin):
weakly to strongly convex (0); straight or slightly concave (1)

29. Psammophore (development):
absent to very weak (0); moderately developed (1); strongly developed, with long ammochaetae forming a basketlike structure beneath the head (2)

30. Maxillary palps (number of segments):
4 (0); 5 (1)

31. Labial palps (number of segments):
3 (0); 4 (1)

32. Color of head:
yellow or red to reddish brown (0); black to blackish brown (1)

B. ALITRUNK CHARACTERS

33. Pronotal declivity (length):
    short (0); long (1)

34. Thoracic rugae (coarseness):
    coarse (0); fine (1)

35. Thoracic rugae (dorsal reticulation):
    absent or very sparse (0); conspicuous and extensive (1)

36. Humeri (shape):
    rounded (0); angular (1)

37. Femur of forelegs (shape):
    strongly incrassate (swollen) (0); not incrassate or only weakly incrassate (1)

38. Mesopropodeal depression:
    absent or inconspicuous (0); conspicuous (1)

39. Propodeum (basal face):
    steeply inclined (0); almost horizontal (1)

40. Propodeal spines:
    present (0); absent (1)

41. Propodeal spines (connecting keel):
    keel absent or represented at best by a ruga at extreme base (0); conspicuous keel present (1)

42. Metasternal flanges (development):
    massive (0); moderately developed (1); absent or very weak (2)

43. Color of alitrunk:
    yellow or red to reddish brown (0); black to blackish brown (1)

44. Setae (color):
    clear (0); dark (brownish yellow to blackish) (1)

45. Setae (shape):
    thin or fine (0); thick or coarse (1)

C. PEDICEL CHARACTERS

46. Node of petiole (shape, in dorsal view):
    elongate, bullet-shaped to almost rectangular (0); not strongly elongated but robust, the sides converging posteriorly and with a constriction (1); almost oval (2)

47. Node of petiole (rugosity):
    ordered in decreasing density: (0); (1); (2)

48. Node of petiole (areolation):
    ordered in decreasing density: (0); (1); (2)
49. Node of petiole (anterior nipple):
    absent (0); present (1)
50. Peduncle of petiole (ventral process):
    absent or very weak (0); moderately developed or with some
    variation between extremes (1); strongly developed (2)
51. Peduncle of petiole (setae, near region associated with ven-
    tral process when present):
    setae absent (0); setae present (1)
52. Peduncle of petiole (dorsolateral groove near origin of node):
    groove absent (0); groove present (1)
53. Node of postpetiole (rugosity):
    ordered in decreasing density: (0); (1); (2)
54. Node of postpetiole (areolation):
    ordered in decreasing density: (0); (1)
55. Node of postpetiole (shape, in dorsal view):
    not robust (0); robust (conspicuously wider than long) (1)
56. Postpetiole (ventral process):
    absent or weakly developed (0); strongly developed (1)

D. GASTER CHARACTERS

57. Basal segment of gaster (rugae, dorsal surface):
    absent (0); confined to base near insertion of postpetiole (1);
    covering most or all of segment (2)
58. Basal segment of gaster (dorsal sculpture, excluding rugae):
    surface mostly smooth and shiny (0); surface shagreened (1);
    surface areolate, at least near insertion of postpetiole (2)
59. Color of gaster:
    yellow or red to reddish brown (0); black to blackish brown
    (1)

E. WORKER POLYMORPHISM AND SIZE

60. Worker size class(es):
    monomorphic (0); weakly polymorphic (1); strongly poly-
    morphic (2)
61. Worker length:
    small (usually 4–6 mm) (0); large (usually 6 mm or longer)(1)

II. Female Reproductive Caste

A. ALITRUNK CHARACTERS

62. Alitrunk contour (dorsal surface, in profile):
    outline uneven due to distinctly elevated scutellum (o); outline even, scutellum not distinctly elevated (1)

63. Wing venation (cubital cell of forewing, modal state, obtained variously from both sexes) (for details see Cole [1968], pl. I, fig. 1, and table, p. 26):
    type A (o); type B (1); type C (2); type D or E (3)

B. GASTER CHARACTERS

64. Stem of furcula of sting apparatus (development):
    stem absent or weak (o); stem moderately developed (1); stem long and prominent (2)

C. REPRODUCTIVE CASTE MORPHOLOGY

65. Female reproductive caste (morphology):
    typical gyne (o); ergatogyne or intercaste (1)

III. Males

A. CEPHALIC CHARACTERS

66. Occipital margin (keel):
    conspicuous keel present (o); keel absent (1)

67. Vertex (shape):
    not flattened (o); flattened (1)

68. Antenna (scape length, exclude pedicel in comparisons):
    shorter than combined lengths of first two flagellum segments (short) (o); longer than combined lengths of first two flagellum segments (long) (1)

69. Antenna (scape, pilosity):
    scape without numerous long hairs (o); scape with numerous long hairs (1)

70. Antenna (first flagellum segment, length):
    less than 4–5 times the length of pedicel (short) (o); 4–5 times longer than pedicel (long) (1)

71. Mandible (number of teeth):

maximum number of teeth 4 (0); both 4 and 5 teeth reported
(1); minimum number of teeth 5 (2)

72. Mandible (contour of basal margin):
not concave (0); concave (1)

B. ALITRUNK CHARACTERS

73. Color of alitrunk:
yellow to brown (0); black to blackish brown (1)

74. Luster of alitrunk:
shiny (0); dull (1)

75. Mayrian furrow (development):
deep (0); absent or indistinct (1)

76. Forewing (pilosity):
hairy (0); not hairy (1)

77. Alitrunk pilosity:
setae short, sparse (0); setae long, dense (1)

C. GASTER CHARACTERS

78. Ninth sternite (lateral processes):
processes absent (0); processes present (1)

IV. Ecology and Nest Structure

79. Piney habitat preference:
no restriction to, or preference for, piney habitats (0); restricted to, or preferring, piney habitats (1)

80. Nest superstructure:
mature nest always or usually without gravel or pebble pavement on mound (0); mature nest always or usually with gravel
or pebble pavement on mound (1)

V. Miscellaneous: Character Used Only in Social Parasite Analysis

81. Gyne (dorsum of petiole):
dorsum of petiole without median longitudinal furrow (0);
dorsum of petiole with median longitudinal furrow (1)

VI. Ecological and Behavioral Characters Not Used in Phylogeny Reconstruction

82. Biome preference:
    restricted to or usually found in mesic forests (0); usually found in such mesic habitats as tropical and subtropical grasslands (1); typically found in semiarid to arid habitats (e.g., scrub, dry grassland, desert) (2)

83. Altitude preference:
    never or uncommonly found in montane/high altitude habitats (0); restricted to or usually found in montane/high altitude habitats (1)

84. Soil preference:
    avoiding or not preferring sand (0); restricted to or preferring sand (1)

85. Nest microhabitat:
    always or usually concealed (e.g., beneath litter, stones, or among vegetation) (0); always or usually exposed (1)

86. Nest depth (mature colonies):
    shallow (app. 1 meter or less) (0); deep (greater than 1 meter) (1)

87. Foraging behavior (mature colonies):
    individual (solitary) only (0); individual only or both individual and group (in files along trunk trails) (1); both individual and group (2)

88. Foraging schedule:
    primarily diurnal (0); both nocturnal and diurnal (1)

89. Colony size (mature):
    small (tens to hundreds) (0); large (over one thousand) (1)

90. Diet:
    seeds (if consumed at all) minor part of diet (0); seeds commonly consumed, but arthropods and other items are significant part of diet (1); diet consists almost entirely of seeds (2)

91. Aggression:
    does not sting readily (0); stings readily (1)

92. Defense posture:
    disturbed ants do not become motionless and open jaws in direction of disturbance (0); disturbed ants become motionless and open jaws in direction of disturbance (1)

93. Nest plugging:
    nest not plugged as part of daily routine (0); nest plugged as part of daily routine (1)

94. Colony emigration:

colony emigration (relocation) common (frequently several times per year) (0); colony emigration rare (usually less than once per year) (1)

95. Gyny level:
monogynous (0); at least occasionally polygynous (1)

96. Time of nuptial flight:
morning (0); afternoon or evening (1)

97. Mating site:
on low or flat ground (0); on elevated objects (e.g., trees, hills, poles) (1)

TABLE A3.1.

CHARACTER (DATA) MATRIX FOR HARVESTER ANT SPECIES
WITH A WORKER CASTE

There is a total of ninety-seven characters. Characters 1 through 80 were used to reconstruct the phylogeny of these harvester ants. The evolution of characters 82 through 97 was analyzed in the light of the resulting evolutionary tree. The out-group or comparison species is *Hylomyrma reitteri*. It provides a root or base for the tree. See figure 6.1 for the results. The two social parasite species were accommodated by a separate analysis, using the data of table A3.2. A question mark in the matrix indicates uncertainty due to inapplicability, variability, borderline cases, polymorphism, or an unknown condition.

H. reitteri

00000000200001100070000007000000000000000000000001000001001000007700001010000007007007070????????????

E. abdominalis

00000002000002210000001007010000001000701001120002010011100001770?????????07?007007007070???2???????

E. angustus

000000020000720100001011700101110010000000101120120120110010017707?????????07700700100070?????0??

E. brevibarbis

0000000707010111210701170100701100170100110101117777720127000010107700100770170007007217710712107????

E. cunicularius

01000000000077101170000100701000000101110070011107120120700100107701010007011000707777070070701107????

E. imberbiculus

0000000020000011001000100701000000100000100111010201101107000101701000101100000072777001010007710?

E. laevigatus

010000070700070201000011100701011117770007000110122070022110010077070???????????????07007071770?????????

E. laevinodis

0000000100000011001000100?010000?010000?0100001?00101210201211100000?????????????????00?201?????????????

E. mayri

01001002?0010?00100000200?010001?01010?00011100?12010?01221010??10101????1?00??0?20?00000000?0???

E. naegelii

000000020000002100000010 0?000000001001?010011?010201001110000???00100010?1000?00?10?100?01??????

E. odoratus

00000010300002010000102 10??101100??000000001 0022100?221100000???00?0??1?1110???00?00??00?0?00?????

E. pima

00000001 0000?21100100010 0?010000001 10000100111 100101201101000121001001201 1000000?20??0000?00?????

E. saucius

?00000000000000010000001 00?000000001 0000000011 201 1201211 100000????????????????00?20?0?????20??????

E. schmitti

000000010000110100000010 0?01000??010000000?1 121002012011 0??00???0????????????00???????????1??????

E. sylvestris

00000002100002011000001 00?000??00010001010000001 12010111 100?0?????????????????0??0??0????0?????????

E. tenuipubens

00000?0200000221 0?0000100?010000?010001010011 2000201 1011 00000???????????????????00??????????????

P. anzensis

0000020021001121001012 1000?012000100011 01?2001 11000002010010 01?????????????????0??2000???0????????

P. apache

1011101031110030010121221010200011001001?100111102102011010010310101100010111 10002??11?00101?????

P. atratus

00000001000?1220010111001001200100111010011011 00020000111010 1?????????????????00?2?????????????

P. badius

01000000000011220010111201001200000001001?10011001100100000102103101010020111 10100?201 1120110010000

P. barbatus

10111000?111012001112121111020001??01010010011?002101011010010300101102000111 10112?01121121001010

P. bicolor

10111000211?022?01102110 1?10200011000010010011 100210101011 01?0103001011000101111 1000201102?1?01??0??

P. bigbendensis

1011101031111111001112 1000?10200011001011?100111102102110010 01?????????????????00?2?0????????????

P. bispinosus

00000001 0001?02001100120 0?001??0101?10?002001?0?0200?0110100 10??001000?011000?00?1??1?0?????????

P. brevispinosus

00000000010111220010?1212 01001200010001 0???1001100100110110 100102001011 02100?11100?20110??0?00?????

P. bruchi

1011101010 1?002101101120 0?001?0010011000012 001 00002000?0110?011????????????????00?10?????????????

P. californicus

00000200?10112100101210010012 00010001101?1001 111 110?200001?01002010110001 0?11100?2?11?0112 1010?01

PHYLOGENY RECONSTRUCTION 165

P. carbonarius

?0000000000?112001011100?0002001001110001110110102000111221 01???0?????????????????00????????0???????

P. catanlilensis

000000002000012200101110010002??100111000011011000200001122001????????????????????00?2?????????????????

P. coarctatus

?01110?0201?0121011011210?00100010?1100002001010020 0?011010210??0?????????????????00?100?10?02????0?1

P. comanche

00000200001012?001012100110020001000110001001101110?101?010010?20101100000?11100?2011?0011001?0?1

P. desertorum

101110001 11?022001112110101020001?001?100100111002102 01?01001030010110?01011110002?11?2002000??11

P. guatemaltecus

00100002000112200100011 00?01200010110001?0011101020111 1100000???0?????????????????00?2?11????2???????

P. huachucanus

000000010000122001111 11100?001000?010001 0?100110112001 1110000013100100120 11?00000?2100???0100??1??

P. inermis

0000000200001120010001100?00200000111001?200100?0201?00101001????????????????????00?2??10???2???????

P. laticeps

100000011?0?102001011100?002000?01?10?002001?01020001101?01???1????????????????00?2111???0???????

P. lobatus

?01110?01010002?010011200?00100010?1100001001010020010110101 1????????????????????00?10010???2???????

P. longibarbis

000001010?0?122001011100?0002??0001?101?0??0110102000111 22?010??000000100100 0?00?21?1???0???????

P. magnacanthus

000?0200110112?00101210010012000110011 01?100112010002011010000120101101000111100?2011?000200?????

P. marcusi

10111010201000210110112 1?00010?010110000010010000200101010010??00100??011001?00?211000?02????1??

P. maricopa

?00?0200010?1210010121101000200 01?00110?01001120110020 1?010010020101101 0?01110??2??1?001?10???01

P. meridionalis

?00000000011120011111000?002???001110100110110001000011 12?01?????????????????00?2????????????????

P. micans

10111000201?012?011?11210?001000101 1?00001001000020010110101 1????????????????????00??0?10??02???????

P. montanus

000001000101122001012110100120001 0?0110001001110100010110100 10??011?10100011 1?10?21?1000111 0???1?

P. occidentalis

000000000101122001012120110120001000111001001110100 0?011010010100101102100111101021011111110110?1

P. pronotalis

00000002000?12200101110010002001001110000110110002000011 00001?????????????????00?21?????????????????

P. rastratus

1000000000001?20010111?00?002000001110100010110002000011 22001???0?????????????????00?2???0??0????????

166   APPENDIX 3

P. rugosus

10?00000111101200111212111110200?10101110011?011??0210?01101?0103001011020001111011121?1111111 10?1010

P. salinus

00000100010112?00101212010012000100011000100011?0110??011010010?00101101 0?0?111???211112012?0?10?1

P. snellingi

10001200100?122001?12100110 12??010001111?01001111 11001010000011?????????????????o??201?????????????

P. subdentatus

0000000000 10112200101212010012000100010000100110012001011010010200101101110?11100?211????0200?????

P. subnitidus

00000100?101122001012110100120001000111001001110100001011010010100101101010?11100?21111111110???0?

P. tenuispina

1011100021 1?00200111212210102000110010100100111001102 01?01001?????????????????o0?20???2012?0?????

P. texanus

10111010211100300111212210102000 11001??1?10011100210201?01 00103?01011000101 11?0012?01?0?020???0??

P. theresiae

0000000010 0?122001011100 0?012??00011100?020011010200011110000?????????????????o???o?????????????

P. uruguayensis

00000000000??200110011 00?002000101??0000200100002 0??0110100 1?????????????????o0??0??1??02????o??

P. vermiculatus

0000000?0?001?200101 11?0?000200?001110?00??0110?0?000?11???01???001000000 1000?00????100?02???????

P. wheeleri

1011100011001210111 111221110200011001010010011100210101101010010??010110?010111?0112 0?1?2?1?10?????

Species B

00000100210112100101210010002??0110 0100 1?10011210000210000?00??010110?0001 11?0??21?????????????

CHARACTER (DATA) MATRIX FOR THE
SOCIAL PARASITES (INQUILINES)

The two social parasites, which lack a worker caste, are *P. anergismus* and *P. colei,* members of the *P. barbatus* species complex. All members of the species complex with known sexuals were included in this table and in the analysis since it is clear that the social parasites belong to that group.

There is a total of eighty-one characters used in this subanalysis, and these were scored for the reproductive female and the male. The species complex is so well established that *P. occidentalis,* a close relative, was used as the out-group in this subanalysis. See figure 6.10 for the results. A question mark in the matrix indicates uncertainty due to inapplicability, variability, borderline cases, polymorphism, or an unknown condition.

P. occidentalis

000000000101122001112120?10?2000?00????001001110110010110?001010010110210011111010

P. anergismus

1011101021110220010121200?102000110110110?1?1?001011111021011110000003001011020001101 0?1

P. apache

101110103111013001112122101020000?10?0??1?100111101102111010010310101100010111100 0

P. barbatus

101?1000211101200111212111?02000?10????001001110210?11101001030010110200011110 11

P. bicolor

1011100021 1?02200111212010 1?200?110?1??001001101011011101001030010110001011110 00

P. colei

10111010210002200101212 10?1?2000110?1??001011?1000101011000003?010110200011 0?0?1

P. desertorum

10111010211?0220011121101010200011 0?????001001111021?11110?0000300101100010111100 0

P. rugosus

10101000211?0220011121211100200 1?10????00110 11?101?0?1110??0103001011020?01111011

P. texanus

1011101021110130011121221010200 0?1?????1?100111102102111010010?? 010110011011 1?001

P. wheeleri

101110002111012001112121111 02??0110?1??001001 111021011110000 10??0101101000 111?011

Appendix 4

A New Harvester Ant

When a new species is discovered, its description must be formal and technical. Almost nothing is known about the biology of this new harvester ant except that it lives in the sand dunes of Baja California. See figures A4.1, A4.2, and A4.3.

Pogonomyrmex snellingi Taber new species

1. Distribution: Mexico
2. Habitat preference: sand dunes at 0–8 m elevation
3. Type material: this species is known from six workers collected by Roy R. Snelling, for whom it is named

Description

The jaws of this species are so distinctive that the insect can be described as the most unusual member of its genus in North America. Nothing is known of the biology of this myrmicine ant except that six workers were collected in 1977 among sand dunes at low elevation in Baja California. It has been kept in the Los Angeles County Natural History Museum (LACNHM).

The description of the new species follows the terminology and abbreviations of Cole (1968), with modifications by Snelling (1981):

A4.1 *A new harvester ant species.* Pogonomyrmex snellingi *of Baja California, in lateral view (worker).*

A4.2 *Snelling's harvester in dorsal view (worker).*

CI (cephalic index) = (HW [head width])(100/HL [head length])

EL (eye length) = maximum length of compound eye in lateral view

EW (eye width) = maximum width of compound eye in lateral view

HL = length of head in full-face view, from occiput to anteriormost tip of clypeus

HW = maximum width of head in full-face view, excluding the eyes

A4.3 The unique jaws of Snelling's harvester. They look much like those of Hylomyrma and are perhaps a throwback or atavism of evolution.

OI (ocular index) = (EL)(100/HL)

PNL (petiolar node length) = length of the node of the petiole in lateral view

PNW (petiolar node width) = maximum width of petiole node in dorsal view

PPL (postpetiole length) = maximum length of postpetiole in dorsal view

PPW (postpetiole width) = maximum width of postpetiole in dorsal view

SI (antenna scape index) = (SL)(100/HW)

SL (antenna scape length) = maximum length of scape, exclusive of condyle

WL (Weber's length) = length of alitrunk in lateral view, from the anterior declivity of the pronotum to the tip of the metasternal lobe

HOLOTYPE (worker caste): Mexico, Baja California, 8 km N Guerrero Negro, altitude 0–8 m; sand dunes, 24 August 1977, R. Snelling (collector) (Holotype location and designation: LACNHM Taber/1).

DESCRIPTION: CI 114.3, EL 0.46 mm, EW 0.28 mm, HL 1.47 mm, HW 1.68 mm, OI 31, PNL 0.49 mm, PNW 0.35 mm, PPL 0.49 mm, PPW 0.60 mm, SI 75, SL 1.26 mm, WL 1.82 mm.

Mandible with seven teeth; apical tooth longest; subapical about equal in length to first basal; second basal (middle tooth) half or less than half the length of first basal; third basal a little longer than subapical and first basal; penultimate tooth length less than or equal to second basal; ultimate tooth strongly offset, about equal in length to subapical, separated from penultimate tooth by a large gap; basal margin of mandible short and almost straight. Dentary margin of mandible not transverse as in all congeners, but oblique, as in *Hylomyrma* Forel. Base of antenna moderately developed, but rather large for a member of the *P. californicus* species complex; basal flange thin; lip weak and curved distad; point weak. Longitudinal cephalic rugae diverging from frontal lobes to occiput, coarseness and spacing of cephalic rugae moderate in comparison with the extremes displayed within the genus; interrugal areolation distinct but not presenting a beaded appearance; circumocular whorls present (common feature in *P. californicus* complex); in lateral view, eye situated approximately in the center of the side of the head; frontal area shallow; lateral lobe of clypeus without projection below antenna fossa. Mesopropodeal depression weak, propodeum with small tubercles, but no spines; rugae of thoracic dorsum coarse, interrugal spaces shining; apex of petiolar node rounded, nipple absent; ventral process of anterior peduncle of petiole weak, the process lacking setae (setae present in *P. barbatus* species complex); ventral process of postpetiole node weak; dorsal rugae of petiolar node sparse and confined to posterior half, surface of node shagreened; a very few rugae on dorsum of postpetiolar node, these confined to extreme posterior of node, the surface of the node shagreened. Dorsum of gaster very lightly shagreened. Setae of head, alitrunk and gaster coarse and clear; psammophore well developed. Body color dark reddish brown.

PARATYPES (worker caste): Five specimens, with same collection data as holotype (location and designation of paratypes: LACNHM Taber/2, Taber/3; MCZ [Museum of Comparative Zoology (Harvard)] Taber/4; USNM [United States National Museum] Taber/5; personal collection of the author Taber/6).

VARIATIONS IN PARATYPE SERIES: CI 100.0–119.0, EL 0.35–0.42 mm, EW 0.25–0.28 mm, HL 1.47–1.65 mm, HW 1.65–

1.75 mm, OI 23.4–26.7, PNL 0.46–0.53 mm, PNW 0.35–0.39 mm, PPL 0.42–0.49 mm, PPW 0.56–0.63 mm, SI 62.7–65.2, SL 1.05–1.12 mm, WL 1.75–1.89 mm.

The propodeal armature varies from very short spines to a complete absence of either spines or tubercles. The paratypes are otherwise similar to the holotype.

DIAGNOSIS: The oblique dentary margin of the mandible (similar to that of *Hylomyrma* Forel) is sufficient for the identification of this species, as all congeners have a roughly transverse margin. Furthermore, no other *Pogonomyrmex* species has the following combination of characters: distinct gap between the ultimate and penultimate mandibular teeth, offset ultimate tooth, short basal mandibular margin, and circumocular whorls. The oblique dentary margin and the presence of circumocular whorls readily distinguish this ant from both *Pogonomyrmex apache* Wheeler and *Pogonomyrmex occidentalis* (Cresson).

DISTRIBUTION: Known only from the type locality.

ETYMOLOGY OF SPECIFIC EPITHET: The new species is dedicated to Roy R. Snelling, accomplished hymenopterist and collector of the ant named in his honor.

DISCUSSION: *Pogonomyrmex snellingi* belongs to the *P. californicus* species complex and is most closely related to *Pogonomyrmex comanche* Wheeler. The species appear as sister taxa in the phylogeny of the genus, sharing as synapomorphies a basal mandibular tooth that is at least slightly offset, and only a moderate amount of areolation on the dorsum of the petiolar node. The dorsum of this node is flattened in *P. comanche* but it is not flattened in *P. snellingi*. Both species occur only in sand, but the distributions of these two ants are widely separated.

Glossary

ADAPTIVE RADIATION: A striking proliferation of species allowed by the evolution of new characteristics or behaviors, often occurring as new habitats are invaded. For example, the proliferation of harvester ant species in western North America appears to be an adaptive radiation allowed by the evolution of their powerful defensive sting and their invasion of dry grasslands with plentiful seeds to store in the nest.

ALITRUNK: The region between but not including the head and the narrow waist of the ant. It only appears to be the familiar insect thorax, because in ants it actually includes part of the abdomen. *See* PROPODEUM.

AMMOCHAETAE: The setae, or hairs, that comprise the beard of many harvester ants.

AREOLATION: A pattern on the surface of the ant that appears to be caused by punctures or holes, but upon microscopic examination is seen to be caused by tiny depressions or craters. Useful for identification.

ASPIRATOR: A simple suction device consisting of a large vial with a rubber stopper pierced by two metal or glass tubes. One tube is bent. The ant will be sucked into the vial through it. The other tube is straight and has a flexible rubber hose or tube attached to it. The collector will place the open end of this rubber tube into the mouth and inhale sharply, drawing the ant into the bent tube and hence into the vial (see fig. 6.4). A gauze or cheesecloth filter is always inserted into the flexible tube, especially when aspirating stinging ants.

AUTOTOMY: The loss or shedding of a limb or appendage, such as the stinger of a honeybee or some harvester ants or the tail of certain lizards.

BARBATOLYSIN: A proteinlike molecule in the venom of the red harvester that causes the rupture of human red blood cells.

BIFURCATION: A division from one stem or branch into two. For example, there is a bifurcation in the letter Y. Evolutionary trees have branches that typically arise from bifurcation or forking in this manner.

BIOGEOGRAPHY: The study of the geographical distribution of living things and how they came to be distributed in their particular ways.

CALLOW: An ant that has emerged from the pupal stage so recently that its exoskeleton has not yet hardened and darkened. A red harvester ant is yellow until its exoskeleton becomes firm.

CASTES: For harvester ants, the different structural and/or behavioral types within the female gender. These are the reproductive queen, or gyne, caste and the sterile worker caste. Since there is really only one kind of male, the term is usually not applied to that sex.

CEPHALIC: Pertaining to the head.

CHARACTER: As used here, a character is an observable feature of a species or genus. Harvester ants have anatomical, behavioral, and ecological characters. For example, head width is an anatomical character; some harvester ant species have wide heads, others have narrow heads. The manner of defense is a behavioral character; some harvesters sting readily, others attempt to hide. Habitat is an ecological character; some harvesters dwell in pine forests, whereas others are never found in pine forests.

CHARACTERISTIC: *See* CHARACTER.

CHARACTER-OPTIMIZATION PROCEDURE: A technical method of determining the most likely evolutionary history of individual characters, based upon the relationships of the various species that possess them, as shown in an evolutionary tree (*see* MAPPING CHARACTERS). Very simple cases can be determined by casual inspection without the aid of a computer. For example, one can easily see by looking at an evolutionary tree of vertebrates constructed, for example, from gene sequence data, that milk production has evolved only once, in the common ancestor of all mammals.

CHIRALITY: Just as people can be right-handed or left-handed, certain molecules can have a particular structural component on one side or the other, much like mirror images.

CHITIN: A modified sugar that partly comprises the (external) skeleton of insects.

CHROMOSOMES: The structures in the nucleus that carry the genes. Humans normally have forty-six. The most commonly observed number among harvester species is thirty-two.

CIRCUMOCULAR: Surrounding the eye.

CLADE: A portion of an evolutionary tree consisting of two or more species and their common ancestor(s). For example, in figure 6.1, *Pogonomyrmex apache, P. bigbendensis, P. texanus,* and two hypothetical ancestors form a clade. One hypothetical ancestor is represented by the perpendicular line that forms a T-shape by branching to *P. texanus* and to the second hypothetical ancestor. The modern descendants of that second ancestor are *P. apache* and *P. bigbendensis*.

CLADISTICS: An approach to the determination of species relationships and classification based upon the possession of shared, derived characters. For example, the ability to produce milk has evolved only once, in the common ancestor of all mammals. When it appeared it was novel, or "derived," and has been shared since that time by all the descendants of that animal. Such a character sets the mammals apart as a well-defined set of related species. Some characters could not be used to set the mammals apart from all other animals. For example, the possession of a backbone is something that reptiles, birds, amphibians, and fishes also possess. The backbone is not a feature that first appeared with the mammals; it is more primitive. *See* SHARED, DERIVED CHARACTER.

CLYPEAL LOBES: Projections present on the head of some harvester ants, just in front of the point where the antennae join the head.

CLYPEUS: A portion of an ant's head, just behind the jaws.

CONGENERS: Members of the same genus. All pogos are congeners. All ephebos are congeners.

CONVOLUTED GLAND: An abdominal gland that synthesizes venom.

COPE'S RULE: A generalization for certain groups of animals, claiming that species become larger in size over time. In a broad sense, this is true of the harvester ants.

CROP: Part of the digestive tract of ants. In some ants, liquid food is stored here and regurgitated to other members of the colony. It has a reduced role in harvesters.

DENTARY MARGIN: The tooth-bearing edge of the mandible.

DIAGNOSTIC CHARACTER: A character that, by itself, is sufficient for identification. For example, of the harvester ants discussed here, only the workers of the genus *Pogonomyrmex* have a well-developed beard. Of *Pogonomyrmex*, only the Comanche harvester has a strongly flattened petiolar node. This node is the top part of the first segment of the waist.

DISPERSAL: The movement of animals from one place to another, resulting in an increase in the range or distribution of the species, at least temporarily.

DISTAD: Located toward the farthest, or distal end.

DUFOUR'S GLAND: A gland in the abdomen that dispenses a homing chemical that is used to mark the position of the nest.

ECOLOGICAL RELEASE: A condition that allows a species to alter its anatomy or behavior due to the lack of competition from other species.

ELAIOSOME: An oil-rich seed appendage. Certain harvesters collect seeds with elaiosomes, bring them home to the nest, remove and eat the elaiosome, and throw the rest of the seed away. The seed has thus been dispersed and can germinate at a distance from competing plants of the same species.

EMERY'S RULE: A generalization that socially parasitic ants or inquilines are closely related to their host species. In its strictest interpretation the parasite and host would be closest relatives. In this strict sense, parasitic harvesters violate Emery's Rule. In a broader sense, it is satisfied.

EMMET: An archaic synonym of "ant."

EPHEBOS: Shorthand for members of the genus *Ephebomyrmex.*

ERGATOGYNES: Reproductive females that have characters in between those of a typical harvester queen and a typical harvester worker. It is the normal condition for several harvester species.

ESTERASE: An enzyme that breaks down esters, molecules formed from the reaction between an alcohol and an acid.

EUCHARITID: A wasp of the family Eucharitidae. Common names are often obtained from family names in this fashion.

EVOLUTION: As used here, the origin of species and the changes in the characteristics of those species over geological time.

EXOSKELETON: An external skeleton. The skeleton of insects is on the outside of the body, not on the inside like that of a human.

FLAGELLUM: Used here to refer to a distal part of the antenna, excluding both the scape (first segment) and the pedicel (second segment).

FORMIC ACID: A chemical found in some, but not all, ants. Harvesters appear to lack this acid.

4-METHYL-3-HEPTANONE: A molecule secreted by the mandibular gland of harvester ants. It spreads alarm throughout the colony and also calls winged harvester ants to the mating grounds.

FURCULA: A Y-shaped structure.

GAMMA RAYS: High-energy radiation that harms many plants and animals more readily than it harms harvester ants.

GASTER: The part of an ant behind the waist. The rounded back end.

GENERIC RANK: The rank of a genus. The various categories used in classification have different ranks. The highest ranking animal category is the kingdom, because it includes all animals and therefore all genera and all species within genera. The genus is a low-ranking category because it includes only subgenera and species. *Pogonomyrmex* has generic rank because it is a genus. *Pogonomyrmex comanche* has species rank because it is a species.

GENUS: A category of classification. Humans comprise the species *Homo sapiens,* of the genus *Homo.* The harvester ants comprise two genera (plural of genus). These genera are *Pogonomyrmex* and *Ephebomyrmex.*

GROUP FORAGING: A search for prey, whether it be animal food or seeds, in which workers use a system of trails to fan out into the area surrounding the nest. *See* INDIVIDUAL FORAGING.

GYNANDROMORPH: An individual that has structural characteristics of the reproductive female (queen) and the male but is not capable of functioning in both sexual roles. *See* HERMAPHRODITE.

GYNE: Another name for a reproductive female. Egg-laying queens are gynes, as are virgin (unmated) queens. "Queen" can be an awkward term because it is sometimes used for the reproductively capable female caste, even if the individual in question has not mated yet, has not left the nest of her birth, and therefore has not begun a nest of her own.

HABITUS: A term meaning "general appearance."

HEMOLYTIC AGENTS: Molecules or chemicals that cause red blood cells to burst.

HERMAPHRODITE: An individual that can function as both male and female. No such individuals have been found among the harvester ants. It is the normal condition for earthworms. *See* GYNANDROMORPH.

HOLOTYPE: A particular individual specified as the type specimen of a species. *See* TYPE SPECIMEN(S) and PARATYPE.

HOMOPLASY: A condition that occurs when two species (for example) have the same character even though they did not inherit it from a common ancestor. It seems to show relationship but does not, because the character arose separately in the evolutionary histories of the two lineages. That is why homoplasy causes problems for classification, and it is why the analyses of this book used as many characters as possible, to avoid reliance on only one or a few characters that might turn out to be misleading due to homoplasy.

HYALURONIDASE: An enzyme that breaks apart a particular sugar found in animal tissues and thereby allows the injected venom to spread more easily through the victim's body.

INCRASSATE: Swollen.

INDIVIDUAL FORAGING: A search for prey, whether it be animal food or seeds, in which workers do not use a system of trails, but move in a more random manner into the area surrounding the nest. *See* GROUP FORAGING.

IN-GROUP: The set of species of actual interest to the investigator when reconstructing the evolutionary history of a group of species. The in-group here consists of all sixty *Pogonomyrmex* and *Ephebomyrmex* harvester ant species. *See* CLADISTICS, OUT-GROUP, and SHARED, DERIVED CHARACTER.

IN PART: A phrase used in identification keys to inform the user that the species in question is so variable that it had to appear in more than one place in the key. The Maricopa harvester is an example.

INQUILINES: *See* SOCIAL PARASITES.

INTERCASTE: *See* INTERMORPH.

INTERMORPH: A term used for ants that have characteristics of more than one caste. For example, an ergatogyne is one kind of intermorph. It has characteristics of the gyne and the worker. *See* CASTES, ERGATOGYNES, GYNE, and WORKER.

KARYOTYPE: The chromosome set of a species, which is prepared by arranging each chromosome after photographing the entire set through a microscope.

KININ: A type of molecule that causes pain.

LARVA: The stage of a harvester ant that hatches from the egg. The larva is a white grub.

LEKKING GROUND: An area in which males display to females (e.g., the sage grouse) or in which males arrive to begin the mating ritual and call the females with perfumelike molecules that are dispensed into the air (e.g., the harvester ants).

LIPASE: An enzyme that breaks down fats.

MAJORITY RULE CONSENSUS TREE: An approximation that represents something like an average of many equally valid evolutionary trees. Before the objective analyses allowed by computers, evolutionists drew a single evolutionary tree that they believed was the best one. Modern evolutionists often discover more than one valid way to represent the relationships among species with the data they have at hand.

MAJORS: Also called major workers. The largest subcaste of certain harvester ant species. *Pogonomyrmex badius* of North America and *P. coarctatus* of South America have major workers. *See* CASTES and SUBCASTE.

MANDIBULAR GLAND: A gland in the head of harvesters that secretes the alarm pheromone 4-methyl-3-heptanone.

MAPPING CHARACTERS: Placing certain characters (with the species that possess them) in the diagram of an evolutionary tree so that a computer analysis can determine the most likely historical changes of the characters during evolution. Many biologists think it best to determine the evolutionary tree with a set of characters different from those of greatest import or interest, so that circular reasoning is avoided. For example, if the group of animals called "mammals" is given status as a group in an evolutionary tree solely by their common possession of milk glands, it might be unwise to ask next, "Now what does this result tell us about the origin of milk glands in the animal kingdom?" It would not be circular to ask what the tree tells us about the origin of hair, as long as the tree did not depend on that character when it was built up from the data set. When true hair is then mapped as a character onto this tree, we find, even by casual inspection, that it has indeed arisen only once, in the ancestor of all mammals. (This is a simplified example; some biologists believe hair has evolved in other animals). Other people think it is fine to discuss the evolution of characters even if those characters were used to define the tree.

MATING SWARM: The group of mating males and females, sometimes numbering in the thousands. The swarm can assemble on the ground, in trees, or on mountaintops.

MAYRIAN FURROW: A Y-shaped depression on the dorsal surface of the thorax of some male harvester ants.

MESOPROPODEAL DEPRESSION: Found on some harvesters, this groove on the ant's dorsal surface resembles a saddle in its placement.

METASTERNAL FLANGES: Wedges, lobes, or sharp points sometimes found on the propodeum, where they flank the attachment of the waist. "Propodeal lobe" is a better term.

METAPLEURAL GLAND: A gland that is diagnostic for ants. It often secretes antibiotics, but there are no reports of the specific function of this gland among the harvester ants. *See* DIAGNOSTIC CHARACTER.

MINORS: Also called minor workers. The smallest subcaste of the worker caste of certain harvester ant species. *Pogonomyrmex badius* of North America and *P. coarctatus* of South America have a minor subcaste. *See* CASTES and SUBCASTE.

MITOCHONDRIAL DNA SEQUENCES: A portion of DNA used to classify organisms and study their evolutionary history. Like the nucleus of a cell, the mitochondrion (a part of the cell that provides us with energy) contains its own DNA material. A strand of DNA contains a long series of subunits, or building blocks, called bases. A long series of bases is called a sequence. Each base position in the sequence is a character, just as head width or antenna length is a character. Thus, comparisons of sequences between species can be used to classify organisms and to study their evolutionary history. Mitochondrial DNA is passed down only from the mother, unlike nuclear genes.

MOBBING: A defensive attack by a large group of animals, such as when a large group of harvester workers begins to swarm over the body of an attacking horned lizard. Crows mob owls.

MONOPHYLETIC GROUP: A group of species (for example) that contains an ancestor and all of its descendants and nothing more. For example, in the evolutionary tree shown in figure 6.1, the portion of the tree that includes *P. apache, P. bigbendensis,* and *P. texanus* forms a monophyletic group (a line segment between two branching points represents an unknown ancestor; the two hypothetical, presumably extinct ancestors here must be included for formality's sake). Classification should be based upon monophyletic groups. For example, it would not make sense to define a genus of insects that contained only half of the harvester ant species and the fire ant, and nothing more. Such a genus would leave out the second half of the harvester ants (and many other ants as well), all of which are more closely related to the first half than any fire ant is. The quest for monophyletic groups in classification is the source of the often heard claim that birds are actually dinosaurs; some extinct dinosaurs were more closely related to the birds than they were to other dinosaurs. *See* GENUS and CLADE.

MYRMECOLOGIST: Someone who studies ants.

NANITIC: Dwarfish. The first brood of a newly mated queen is often nanitic.

NECROPHORIC: Pertaining to the transportation of dead bodies.

OCCIPUT: The top of the head, the highest point when viewed from the side.

OCELLI: The three small, simple eyes of queens and males. Each one is an ocellus. Compound eyes are different. Each ant has two of these, and they are larger and more readily visible than ocelli.

OCULAR: Pertaining to the eye.

ORTHOGENESIS: A largely abandoned view that evolution follows some plan, perhaps a principle of perfection. One good reason to reject this concept is the fact that over 90 percent of all species that ever lived are now extinct.

OSMOTIC PRESSURE: A measure of the behavior of pure water in a given environment. If a cell has a high salt concentration, it will have a high osmotic pressure, and water will tend to flow into it.

OUT-GROUP: A species or group of species that is used as an aid when re-constructing the evolutionary history of a group of species (*see* IN-GROUP). The out-group is closely related to the species of interest and allows the investigator to determine which characters are primitive and which are derived. Only shared, derived characters are used to build the evolutionary tree according to cladistic principles. The out-group here is the ant *Hylomyrma reitteri*, not a harvester ant at all. *See* CLADISTICS, IN-GROUP, and SHARED, DERIVED CHARACTER.

OVIPOSITOR: Primitively, a tubular egg-laying organ. Ants are unusual because the ovipositor is no longer used for this purpose. The eggs are laid through a different opening in the queen's body. The modified ovipositor is familiar to humans as the venom-carrying stinger of ants, bees, and wasps. Thus, only female insects can sting.

PARASITOID: An organism that is parasitic in part, but not all, of its life cycle.

PARATYPE: A specimen used in addition to the holotype when describing a new species.

PECTINATE: Comblike.

PEDICEL: Two meanings: (1) The waist, consisting of two segments in harvesters, and (2) the second segment of the antenna.

PEDUNCLE: The anterior stalk of the waspish waist of a harvester ant. It attaches to the alitrunk. *See* ALITRUNK.

PETIOLE: The first segment of the waspish waist of harvester ants.

PHOSPHATASE: An enzyme that modifies the structure of certain phosphorus-containing molecules.

PHYLOGENY: An evolutionary tree.

PILOSITY: Long, fine hairs (as opposed to the more abundant and shorter setae).

PLANIDIUM: A legless larva of certain wasps. One such wasp appears to be a parasitoid of the harvester ant *Ephebomyrmex cunicularius*. *See* PARASITOID.

POGOS: Shorthand for members of the genus *Pogonomyrmex*.

POISON GLAND: The abdominal gland that stores the venom of harvester ants.

POLARIZED SUNLIGHT: Sunlight in which the vibration of the electric field is in a common plane.

POLYMORPHISM: The existence of two or more subcastes within the worker caste. *See* CASTES and SUBCASTE.

POSTPHARYNGEAL GLAND: A gland largely, if not entirely, exclusive to ants. It is located in the head and its secretion is used by some species to feed the larvae.

PRONOTUM: An area on the back of an ant, but only the region just behind the head.

PROPODEUM: The part of an ant that connects to the front end of the waist. It only appears to be part of the familiar insect thorax, but it is in fact part of the abdomen. The propodeum bears the spines, when spines are present. *See* ALITRUNK.

PSAMMOPHORE: The beard. Literally, "sand carrier."

PUNCTATION: An older name for areolation. *See* AREOLATION.

PUPA: The stage of development between the white larva (a grub) and the familiar six-legged adult ant.

RAINSHADOW: A dry area produced by coastal mountain ranges.

RECRUITMENT: A summons for nestmates to gather at a food source.

RECRUITMENT PHEROMONE: A chemical stored in the poison gland and secreted to alert other workers to the presence of a food source.

RELICT: As used here, a relatively old species with limited distribution.

ROENTGEN: A unit of radiation exposure measured in terms of the amount of ionized air produced by the radiation.

RUGAE: Wrinkles on the surface of an ant's exoskeleton. Rugae are important in the identification of harvester ant species.

SCAPE: The long, first segment of the antenna. It attaches at its lower end to the surface of the head.

SCIENTIFIC NAME: A two-part technical name for a species. *Pogonomyrmex barbatus* is the scientific name of the red harvester ant.

SCUTELLUM: A part of a plate found on the dorsal surface of the thorax of gynes and males.

SESQUITERPENOID: A class of compounds containing particular arrangements of carbon and hydrogen.

SETAE: The tiny hairlike structures that protrude from the surface of a harvester ant's body.

SEXUALS: The reproductive harvester ants. These are the males and the queens (both the virgin queens and those that have already mated and begun a nest).

SHAGREENED: Roughened, referring to the texture of a surface.

SHARED, DERIVED CHARACTER: The kind of character used in the methods of cladistics to build evolutionary trees by establishing relationships. When a new species appears in evolution, its appearance is accompanied by a derived (novel) character or characters, providing a natural way to study evolution. A shared, derived character is one that indicates a relationship between two or more species that arose after the origin of such a character in their most recent common ancestor. It is called a synapomorphy.

SISTER SPECIES: Two species that are one another's closest relatives. In figure 6.1, *P. apache* and *P. bigbendensis* are sister species.

SOCIAL PARASITES: Species that lack a worker caste and live in the nest of other harvester ant species. *Pogonomyrmex anergismus* and *P. colei* are social parasites.

SPECIES COMPLEX: *See* SPECIES GROUP.

SPECIES GROUP: A monophyletic group of species within a genus. *See* MONOPHYLETIC GROUP and GENUS.

SPERMATHECA: An organ in which the mated queen stores sperm. The sperm can remain viable in the spermatheca for forty years or more.

SPIRACLE VALVE: A structure that can be closed to prevent water loss from the breathing tubes of an insect.

STATOLITH: A mineral structure found in many animals that aids in maintaining balance. Harvester ants do not appear to have them.

STERNAL GLAND: An abdominal gland with unknown function among the harvester ants. Some wasps use it to secrete a substance that repels ants.

STERNITE: A ventral plate of the exoskeleton.

STRIDULATION: The audible movement of one abdominal plate over another. It causes a squeaking noise easily heard by humans when the insect is held close to the ear.

SUBCASTE: One of the size classes within the worker caste of some harvester ant species. *See* MAJORS and MINORS.

SUBGENERIC RANK: A rank or level of classification lower than the genus but higher than the species. For animals, the highest ranking category is the kingdom.

SYMBIONTS: Organisms (not members of the same species) that live together in some way.

SYNAPOMORPHY: *See* SHARED, DERIVED CHARACTER.

TRAIL PHEROMONE: *See* RECRUITMENT PHEROMONE.

TROPHIC EGGS: Eggs that are produced by a species and used by that same species for food.

TRUNK TRAIL: The widest of the trails made or used by group foraging harvester ants.

TUBERCLE: A tiny bump or point.

TYPE SPECIMEN(S): An individual or individuals used in the original description of a new species and designated as such. Many harvester ant type specimens were examined in the preparation of this book, some of them over one hundred years old. *See* HOLOTYPE and PARATYPE.

VENTER: The lower surface.

VERTEX: The upper surface of the head, bordered by the occiput and the more laterally placed compound eyes.

VICARIANCE: The separation of a species into two or more populations by a physical barrier, such as a mountain range or the growth of a forest. Vicariance has been important in the evolution of the harvester ants.

VIRGIN QUEENS: Female harvester ants of the gyne caste that have not yet mated. They will eventually leave their birth nest, mate, shed their wings, and then begin a nest of their own. When they begin laying eggs in their own nest, they become true queens. Since they can't be queens until after mating, the phrase "virgin queens" is an unfortunate one that happens to have wide usage and historical precedent.

WILLISTON'S RULE: A generalization that the number of segments in the body or in appendages tends to become smaller over time. Three *Ephebomyrmex* species have an increased number of segments in certain mouthparts, thereby violating the rule. Evolution appears to follow very few rules of this kind, if any.

WORKER: One of the two female harvester ant castes. The other caste is the gyne or queen caste. All harvester ant workers are sterile females, although workers of the Florida harvester can produce nonviable eggs that are used for food. *See* TROPHIC EGGS.

Bibliography

Attygalle, A. B., and E. D. Morgan. 1985. Ant trail pheromones. In *Advances in insect physiology*, vol. 18, edited by M. J. Berridge, J. E. Treherne, and V. B. Wigglesworth. New York: Academic Press.

Baez, A. M., and G. J. S. Yane. 1979. Late Cenozoic environmental changes in temperate Argentina. In *The South American herpetofauna: Its origin, evolution, and dispersal*, edited by W. E. Duellman. Monograph no. 7. Lawrence: Museum of Natural History, University of Kansas.

Baroni Urbani, C. 1993. The diversity and evolution of recruitment behavior in ants, with a discussion of the usefulness of parsimony criteria in the reconstruction of evolutionary histories. *Insectes Sociaux* 40:233–60.

Benthuysen, J. L., and M. S. Blum. 1974. Quantitative sensitivity of the ant *Pogonomyrmex barbatus* to the enantiomers of its alarm pheromone. *J. Georgia Entomol. Soc.* 9 (4):235–38.

Bernheimer, A. W., L. S. Avigad, and J. O. Schmidt. 1980. A hemolytic polypeptide from the venom of the red harvester ant, *Pogonomyrmex barbatus*. *Toxicon* 18:271–78.

Bernstein, R. A. 1971. The ecology of ants in the Mojave Desert: Their interspecific relationships, resource utilization, and diversity. Ph.D. diss., University of California, Los Angeles.

Berry, E. W. 1923. *Tree ancestors: A glimpse into the past*. Baltimore, Md.: Williams and Wilkins.

Billen, J. P. J., A. B. Attygalle, E. D. Morgan, and D. G. Ollett. 1987. Gas chromatography without solvents: Pheromone studies: The Dufour gland of the ant *Pogonomyrmex occidentalis*. *International Analyst* 1 (March): 3–6.

Blum, M. S., R. E. Doolittle, and M. Beroza. 1971. Alarm pheromones: Utilization in evaluation of olfactory theories. *J. Insect Phys.* 17:2351–61.

Bohart, G. E., and G. F. Knowlton. 1953. Notes on food habits of the western harvester ant (Hymenoptera: Formicidae). *Proc. Entomol. Soc. Wash.* 55 (3):151–53.

Bolton, B. 1994. *Identification guide to the ant genera of the world.* Cambridge: Harvard University Press.

Borth, P. W. 1986. Field evaluation of several insecticides on Maricopa harvester ant (Hymenoptera: Formicidae) colony activity in fallow southwestern Arizona cropland. *J. Econ. Entomol.* 79:1632–36.

Borth, P. W., B. R. Tickes, and G. D. Johnson. 1982. *A preliminary evaluation of Amdro for control of a harvester ant (Pogonomyrmex maricopa Wheeler) in hard red spring wheat.* Forage and Grain Series no. P-57. Tucson: University of Arizona, College of Agriculture.

Bruch, C. 1916. Contribución al estudio de las hormigas de la Provincia de San Luis. *Rev. Mus. La Plata* 23:291–357.

―――. 1923. Estudios mirmecológicos con la descripción de nuevas especies de dípteros (Phoridae) por los Rr. Pp. H. Schmitz y Th. Borgmeier y de una araña (Gonyleptidae) por el Doctor Mello-Leitão. *Rev. Mus. La Plata* 27:172–220.

Buckley, S. B. 1860. *Myrmica (Atta) molefaciens,* "stinging ant," or "mound-making ant," of Texas. *Proc. Acad. Nat. Sci. Phil.* 12:445–47.

Bullock, S. H. 1974. Seed dispersal of *Dendromecon* by the seed predator *Pogonomyrmex. Madrono* 22 (7):378–79.

Burkhalter, L. W. 1965. *Gideon Lincecum, 1793–1874: A Biography.* Austin: University of Texas Press.

Burnham, L. 1978. Survey of social insects in the fossil record. *Psyche* 85 (1):85–133.

Cade, W. H., P. H. Simpson, and O. P. Breland. 1978. *Apiomerus spissipes* (Hemiptera: Reduviidae): A predator of harvester ants in Texas. *Southwest. Entomol.* 3 (3):195–97.

Cadwell, L. L. 1973. Colony formation of the western harvester ant in a chronic gamma radiation field. *Amer. Midland Nat.* 89 (2):446–48.

Carlson, D. M., and J. B. Gentry. 1973. Effects of shading on the migratory behavior of the Florida harvester ant, *Pogonomyrmex badius. Ecology* 54:452–53.

Cazier, M. A., and M. A. Mortenson. 1965. Bionomical observations on myrmecophilous beetles of the genus *Cremastocheilus* (Coleoptera: Scarabaeidae). *J. Kansas Entomol. Soc.* 38 (1):19–44.

Chamberlin, R. V. 1908. Animal names and anatomical terms of the Goshute Indians. *Proc. Acad. Nat. Sci. Phil.* (April):74–103.

Clark, W. H. 1977. Idaho's insect reporter. Moscow: University of Idaho, College of Agriculture, Cooperative Extension Service.

Clark, W. H., and P. L. Comanor. 1973. The use of western harvester ant,

Pogonomyrmex occidentalis (Cresson), seed stores by heteromyid rodents. *Biol. Soc. Nevada Occas. Papers* 34:1–6.

Cole, A. C., Jr. 1934a. An extraordinary mound of the occident ant, *Pogonomyrmex occidentalis* Cresson (Hym.: Formicidae). *Entomol. News* 45:170.

———. 1934b. A brief account of aestivation and overwintering of the occident ant, *Pogonomyrmex occidentalis* Cresson, in Idaho. *Can. Entomol.* 66 (9):193–98.

———. 1963. A preliminary synopsis of the subgenera and complexes of the ant genus *Pogonomyrmex* Mayr in North America. *Symp. Genet. Biol. Ital.* 12:51–59.

———. 1968. Pogonomyrmex *harvester ants: A study of the genus in North America*. Knoxville: University of Tennessee Press.

Cole, B. J., and D. C. Wiernasz. 1997. Inbreeding in a lek-mating ant species, *Pogonomyrmex occidentalis. Behav. Ecol. Sociobiol.* 40:79–86.

Cordier. 1833. Discourse on Latreille's death. *Ann. Soc. Entomol. France* 2:xxiii–iv.

Cowan, F. 1865. *Curious facts in the history of insects*. Philadelphia: J. B. Lippincott and Company.

Crist, T. O., and C. F. Friese. 1993. The impact of fungi on soil seeds: Implications for plants and granivores in a semiarid shrub-steppe. *Ecology* 74 (8):2231–39.

Croizat, L. 1958. The New World. Vol. 1 of *Panbiogeography*. Codicote, Herts., England: Wheldon and Wesley.

Crowe, M. 1997. Treasure of the Sierra Madre. *Nat. Hist.* 106 (3):48–50.

Crowell, H. H. 1963. Control of the western harvester ant, *Pogonomyrmex occidentalis,* with poisoned baits. *J. Econ. Entomol.* 56 (3):295–98.

Crozier, R. H., L. S. Jermiin, and M. Chiotnis. 1997. Molecular evidence for a Jurassic origin of ants. *Naturwissenschaften* 84:22–23.

Darling, K. 1977. *Ants have pets*. Champaign, Ill.: Garrard Publishing.

Davidson, D. W. 1977. Foraging ecology and community organization in desert seed-eating ants. *Ecology* 58:725–37.

Dean, G. A. 1905. The mound-building prairie ant *(Pogonomyrmex occidentalis). Trans. Kansas Acad. Sci.* 19:164–70.

DeMers, M. N. 1993. Roadside ditches as corridors for range expansion of the western harvester ant (*Pogonomyrmex occidentalis* Cresson). *Landscape Ecology* 8 (2):93–102.

DeVita, J. 1979. Mechanisms of interference and foraging among colonies of the harvester ant *Pogonomyrmex californicus* in the Mojave Desert. *Ecology* 60 (4):729–37.

Dorros, A. 1987. *Ant cities*. New York: Thomas Y. Crowell.

Dow, R. P. 1913. The makers of Coleopterous species. *Bull. Brooklyn Entomol. Soc.* 8 (3):37–41.

Eddy, T. A. 1970. Foraging behavior of the western harvester ant, *Pogonomyrmex occidentalis*, (Hymenoptera: Formicidae) in Kansas. Ph.D. diss., Kansas State University.

Elias, S. A., and T. R. Van Devender. 1992. Insect fossil evidence of late Quaternary environments in the northern Chihuahuan Desert of Texas and New Mexico: Comparisons with the paleobotanical record. *Southwest. Nat.* 37 (2):101–16.

Emery, C. 1921. Hymenoptera, fam. Formicidae, subfam. Myrmicinae. In *Genera insectorum*, no. 174, edited by P. Wytsman. Brussels: Louis Desmet-Verteneuil.

Essig, E. O. 1929. *Insects of western North America.* New York: MacMillan.

Evans, H. E. 1962. A review of nesting behavior of digger wasps of the genus *Aphilanthops*, with special attention to the mechanics of prey carriage. *Behaviour* 19:239–60.

———. 1997. The natural history of the Long expedition to the Rocky Mountains, 1819–1820. New York: Oxford University Press.

Evans, H. E., and M. J. West-Eberhard. 1970. *The wasps.* Ann Arbor: University of Michigan Press.

Everitt, J. H., D. E. Escobar, K. R. Summy, M. A. Alaniz, and M. R. Davis. 1996. Using spatial information technologies for detecting and mapping whitefly and harvester ant infestations in south Texas. *Southwest. Entomol.* 21 (4):421–32.

Fales, H. M., T. H. Jones, T. Jaouni, M. S. Blum, and J. O. Schmidt. 1992. Phenylalkenals in ponerine (*Leptogenys* sp.) and myrmicine (*Pogonomyrmex* sp.) ants. *J. Chem. Ecology* 18 (6):847–54.

Fewell, J. H. 1988. Energetic and time costs of foraging in harvester ants, *Pogonomyrmex occidentalis. Behav. Ecol. Sociobiol.* 22:401–408.

Fitzner, R. E., K. A. Gano, W. H. Rickard, and L. E. Rogers. 1979. *Characterization of the Hanford 300 Area Burial Grounds: Task IV—biological transport.* Pacific NW Laboratory, Battelle Memorial Institute, Richland, Wash. Microfiche.

Gallardo, A. 1932. Las hormigas de la República Argentina: Subfamilia Mirmicinas, segunda sección Eumyrmicinae, tribu Myrmicini (F. Smith), género *Pogonomyrmex* Mayr. *An. Mus. Nac. Hist. Nat. Buenos Aires* 37:89–170.

Gemignani, E. V. 1933. La familia Eucharidae (Hymenoptera: Chalcidoidea) en la República Argentina. *An. Mus. Argent. Cienc. Nat. Buenos Aires* 37:477–93.

Gentry, A. H. 1982. Neotropical floristic diversity: Phytogeographical connections between Central and South America, Pleistocene climatic fluctuations, or an accident of the Andean orogeny? *Ann. Missouri Bot. Gard.* 69:557–93.

Gentry, J. B. 1974. Response to predation by colonies of the Florida harvester ant, *Pogonomyrmex badius*. *Ecology* 55:1328–38.

Gentry, J. B., and K. L. Stiritz. 1972. The role of the Florida harvester ant, *Pogonomyrmex badius*, in old field mineral nutrient relationships. *Environ. Entomol.* 1 (1):39–41.

Giezentanner, K. I., and W. H. Clark. 1974. The use of western harvester ant mounds as strutting locations by sage grouse. *Condor* 76 (2):218–19.

Gilbert, H. 1960. Sheridan man conducts survey of ant hills on Wyoming ranges. *Wyoming Stockman-Farmer* 66 (5):29, 63.

Gillis, A. M. 1996. Andean fossils push back the age of origin for modern ecosystems and species' lineages. *Bioscience* 46 (8):570–72.

Goddard, J. 1993. *Physician's guide to arthropods of medical importance.* Boca Raton, Fla.: CRC Press.

Goetsch, W. 1932. Beiträge zur Biologie südamerikanischer Ameisen. I. Teil: Wüstenameisen. *Z. f. Morphol. u. Ökol. d. Tiere* 25:1–30.

———. 1934. Untersuchungen über die zusammenarbeit in Ameisenstaat. *Z. f. Morphol. u. Ökol. d. Tiere* 28:319–401.

———. 1935. Biologie und Verbreitung chilenischer Wüsten-, Steppen-, und Waldameisen. *Zoolog. Jahrb. Syst.* 67 (4):235–318.

Golley, F. B., and J. B. Gentry. 1964. Bioenergetics of the southern harvester ant, *Pogonomyrmex badius*. *Ecology* 45 (2):217–25.

Gordon, D. M. 1984a. The harvester ant (*Pogonomyrmex badius*) midden: Refuse or boundary? *Ecol. Entomol.* 9:403–12.

———. 1984b. The persistence of role in exterior workers of the harvester ant, *Pogonomyrmex badius*. *Psyche* 91 (3/4):251–65.

———. 1988. Nest-plugging: Interference competition in desert ants *(Novomessor cockerelli* and *Pogonomyrmex barbatus). Oecologia* 75:114–18.

———. 1991. Behavioral flexibility and the foraging ecologies of seed-eating ants. *Amer. Nat.* 138 (2):379–411.

Gordon, D. M., and D. Wagner. 1997. Neighborhood density and reproductive potential in harvester ants. *Oecologia* 109:556–60.

Grant, V. 1985. *The evolutionary process.* New York: Columbia University Press.

Grove, F. P. 1947. *Consider her ways.* Vol. 132. Toronto, Ont.: McClelland and Stewart Limited, New Canadian Library.

Harmon, G. 1993. Mating in *Pogonomyrmex badius* (Hymenoptera: Formicidae). *Florida Entomol.* 76 (3):524–26.

Harvester ant migrations. 1970. In *Fundamental nuclear energy research 1969: A supplemental report to the annual report to Congress for 1969 of the US Atomic Energy Commission,* edited by G. T. Seaborg. Washington, D.C.

Heinze, J., B. Hölldobler, and S. P. Cover. 1992. Queen polymorphism in the

North American harvester ant, *Ephebomyrmex imberbiculus. Insectes Sociaux* 39:267–73.

Herms, W. B. 1950. *Medical Entomology.* New York: MacMillan.

Holden, C. 1996. The Vatican's position evolves. *Science* 274:717.

Hölldobler, B. 1970. *Steatoda fulva* (Theridiidae), a spider that feeds on harvester ants. *Psyche* 77 (2):202–208.

———. 1976a. Recruitment behavior, home range orientation, and territoriality in harvester ants, *Pogonomyrmex. Behav. Ecol. Sociobiol.* 1 (1):3–44.

———. 1976b. The behavioral ecology of mating in harvester ants (Hymenoptera: Formicidae: *Pogonomyrmex*). *Behav. Ecol. Sociobiol.* 1 (4):405–23.

———. 1984. The wonderfully diverse ways of the ant. *National Geographic* (June):779–813.

Hölldobler, B., and H. Markl. 1989. Notes on interspecific, mixed colonies in the harvester ant genus *Pogonomyrmex. Psyche* 96 (3/4):237–38.

Hölldobler, B., and E. O. Wilson. 1970. Recruitment trails in the harvester ant *Pogonomyrmex badius. Psyche* 77 (4):385–99.

———. 1990. *The ants.* Cambridge: Harvard University Press, Belknap Press.

———. 1994. *Journey to the ants: A story of scientific exploration.* Cambridge: Harvard University Press, Belknap Press.

Hubrich, J. 1929. Bau und Vorräte argentinischer Ernteameisen. *Wanderversammlung Deutscher Entomologen.*

Hull, D. A., and A. J. Beattie. 1988. Adverse effects on pollen exposed to *Atta texana* and other North American ants: Implications for ant pollination. *Oecologia* 75:153–55.

Hungerford, H. B., and F. X. Williams. 1912. Biological notes on some Kansas Hymenoptera. *Entomol. News* 23 (6):241–60.

Hunt, J. H. 1973. Comparative ecology of ant communities in Mediterranean regions of California and Chile. Ph.D. diss., University of California, Berkeley.

Hunter, W. D. 1912. Two destructive Texas ants. Circular no. 148. Washington, D.C.: USDA Bureau of Entomol.

Hutchins, R. E. 1958. Consider the harvester ant. In *The illustrated library of the natural sciences,* vol. II, edited by E. M. Weyer Jr. New York: Simon and Schuster.

———. 1966. *Insects.* Englewood Cliffs, N.J.: Prentice-Hall.

———. 1967. *The ant realm.* New York: Dodd, Mead, and Company.

Ingham, C. O. 1963. *An ecological and taxonomic study of the ants of the Great Basin and Mohave Desert regions of southwestern Utah.* Ph.D. diss., University of Utah.

Johnson, R. A. 1995. Distribution and natural history of the workerless inquiline ant *Pogonomyrmex anergismus* Cole (Hymenoptera: Formicidae). *Psyche* 101:257–62.

Johnson, R. A., J. D. Parker, and S. W. Rissing. 1996. Rediscovery of the workerless inquiline ant *Pogonomyrmex colei* and additional notes on natural history (Hymenoptera: Formicidae). *Insectes Sociaux* 43:69–76.

Johnson, R. A., S. W. Rissing, and P. R. Killeen. 1994. Differential learning and memory by co-occurring ant species. *Insectes Sociaux* 41:165–77.

Johnston, E. L. 1912. The western harvesting ants. *Guide to Nature* 5 (7):210–14.

Jones, C. R. 1929. Ants and their relation to aphids. *Bull. Colo. Agr. Exp. Sta.* 341.

Keeler, K. H. 1993. Fifteen years of colony dynamics in *Pogonomyrmex occidentalis,* the western harvester ant, in western Nebraska. *Southwest. Nat.* 38 (3):286–89.

Killough, J. R., and A. C. Hull Jr. 1951. Ants denude 90,000 acres in Big Horn Basin. *Wyoming Stockman-Farmer* 57 (6):8.

King, C. L. 1963. *Harvester ant forage utilization studies in the Big Horn Basin of Wyoming.* Cheyenne: Wyoming Game and Fish Commission.

Kleiner, K. 1997. Flies enlisted to fight fire ants. *New Scientist* 153 (2070):6.

Knoch, T. R., S. H. Faeth, and D. L. Arnott. 1993. Endophytic fungi alter foraging and dispersal by desert seed-harvesting ants. *Oecologia* 95:470–73.

Knowlton, G. F. 1953. Harvester ant control. Utah State Agricultural College Extension Circular, no. 198.

———. 1974. Some terrestrial arthropod food of Curlew Valley birds. Utah State University Ecology Center, Terrestrial Arthropod Series, no. 8.

Krebs, A., and B. Benson. 1966. Effects of ^{60}Co-gamma radiation on natural digging and tunneling behavior of the ant *Pogonomyrmex californicus.* *Naturwissenschaften* 53 (5):171.

Kugler, C. 1978. Description of the ergatoid queen of *Pogonomyrmex mayri* with notes on the worker and male (Hymenoptera: Formicidae). *Psyche* 85:169–82.

———. 1984. Ecology of the ant *Pogonomyrmex mayri:* Foraging and competition. *Biotropica* 16 (3):227–34.

Kugler, C., and M. C. Hincapie. 1983. Ecology of the ant *Pogonomyrmex mayri:* Distribution, abundance, nest structure, and diet. *Biotropica* 15 (3):190–98.

Kusnezov, N. 1949. *Pogonomyrmex* del grupo *Ephebomyrmex* en la fauna de la Patagonia (Hymenoptera: Formicidae). *Acta Zool. Lill.* 8:291–307.

———. 1951. El género *Pogonomyrmex* Mayr. *Acta Zool. Lill.* 11:227–333.

———. 1952. Algunos datos sobre la dispersión geográfica de hormigas (Hymenoptera: Formicidae) en la República Argentina. *An. Soc. Cient. Argent.* 153:230–42.

———. 1953. Tendencias evolutivas de las hormigas en la parte austral de Sud América. *Folia Univ. Cochab.* 6:3–210.

———. 1954. Reacciones defensivas y ofensivas en las hormigas. *Folia Univ. Cochab.* 7:55–81.

———. 1959. La fauna de hormigas en el oeste de la Patagonia y Tierra del Fuego. *Acta Zool. Lill.* 17:321–401.

———. 1978. Hormigas Argentinas: Clave para su identificación. Edition prepared by R. Golbach. Tucumán, Argentina: Ministerio de Cultura y Educación Fundación Miguel Lillo.

Lavigne, R. J. 1966. Individual mound treatments for control of the western harvester ant, *Pogonomyrmex occidentalis,* in Wyoming. *J. Econ. Entomol.* 59 (3):525–32.

———. 1969. Bionomics and nest structure of *Pogonomyrmex occidentalis* (Hymenoptera: Formicidae). *Ann. Entomol. Soc. Amer.* 62 (5):1166–75.

Lean, G., D. Hinrichsen, and A. Markham. 1990. *Atlas of the environment (WWF).* New York: Prentice Hall.

Lee, S. H. 1955. The mode of egg dispersal in *Physaloptera phrynosoma* Ortlepp (Nematoda: Spiruroidea), a gastric nematode of Texas horned toads, *Phrynosoma cornutum. J. Parasit.* 41 (1):70–74.

———. 1957. The life cycle of *Skrjabinoptera phrynosoma* (Ortlepp) Schulz, 1927 (Nematoda: Spiruroidea), a gastric nematode of Texas horned toads, *Phrynosoma cornutum. J. Parasit.* 43 (1):66–75.

Lighton, J. R. B., and G. A. Bartholomew. 1988. Standard energy metabolism of a desert harvester ant, *Pogonomyrmex rugosus:* Effects of temperature, body mass, group size, and humidity. *Proc. Nat. Acad. Sci.* 85:4765–69.

Lighton, J. R. B., and D. H. Feener Jr. 1989. A comparison of energetics and ventilation of desert ants during voluntary and forced locomotion. *Nature* 342 (6245):174–75.

Lighton, J. R. B., D. A. Garrigan, F. D. Duncan, and R. A. Johnson. 1993. Spiracular control of respiratory water loss in female alates of the harvester ant *Pogonomyrmex rugosus. J. Exper. Biol.* 179:233–44.

Lincecum, G. 1862. Notice on the habits of the "agricultural ant" of Texas ["stinging ant" or "mound-making ant," *Myrmica (Atta) malefaciens,* Buckley]. *J. Proc. Linn. Soc. London, Zoology* 6:29–31.

———. 1866. On the agricultural ant of Texas *(Myrmica Molefaciens). Proc. Acad. Nat. Sci. Phil.* 18:323–31.

———. 1874. The agricultural ant. *Amer. Nat.* 8 (9):513–17.

McCluskey, E. S. 1992. Periodicity and diversity in ant mating flights. *Comp. Biochem. Physiol.* 103A (2):241–43.

McCook, H. C. 1877. On the vital powers of ants. *Proc. Acad. Nat. Sci. Phil.* 29:134–37.

———. 1879. *The natural history of the agricultural ant of Texas.* Philadelphia: Academy of Natural Sciences of Philadelphia, Lippincott's Press.

———. 1882. *The honey ants of the garden of the gods, and the occident ants of the American plains.* Philadelphia: J. B. Lippincott and Company.

McCoy, E. D., and B. W. Kaiser. 1990. Changes in foraging activity of the southern harvester ant *Pogonomyrmex badius* (Latreille) in response to fire. *Amer. Midland Nat.* 123 (1):112–23.

McGurk, D. J., J. Frost, E. J. Eisenbraun, K. Vick, W. A. Drew, and J. Young. 1966. Volatile compounds in ants: Identification of 4-methyl-3-heptanone from *Pogonomyrmex* ants. *J. Insect Phys.* 12:1435–41.

MacKay, W. P. 1981. A comparison of the nest phenologies of three species of *Pogonomyrmex* harvester ants (Hymenoptera: Formicidae). *Psyche* 88 (1/2):25–74.

———. 1982a. The effect of predation of western widow spiders (Araneae: Theridiidae) on harvester ants (Hymenoptera: Formicidae). *Oecologia* 53:406–11.

———. 1982b. An altitudinal comparison of oxygen consumption rates in three species of *Pogonomyrmex* harvester ants (Hymenoptera: Formicidae). *Physiol. Zool.* 55 (4):367–77.

MacKay, W. P., and S. A. Elias. 1992. Late Quaternary ant fossils from packrat middens (Hymenoptera: Formicidae): Implications for climatic change in the Chihuahuan desert. *Psyche* 99 (2/3):169–84.

MacKay, W. P., and E. E. MacKay. 1984. Why do harvester ants store seeds in their nests? *Sociobiology* 9 (1):31–47.

MacKay, W. P., S. Majdi, J. Irving, S. B. Vinson, and C. Messer. 1992. Attraction of ants (Hymenoptera: Formicidae) to electric fields. *J. Kansas Entomol. Soc.* 65 (1):39–43.

Mallis, A. 1941. A list of the ants of California with notes on their habits and distribution. *Bull. Southern Calif. Acad. Sci.* 40 (2):61–100.

———. 1971. *American entomologists.* New Brunswick, N.J.: Rutgers University Press.

Mandel, R. D., and C. J. Sorenson. 1982. The role of the western harvester ant *(Pogonomyrmex occidentalis)* in soil formation. *Soil Sci. Soc. Amer. J.* 46:785–88.

Mangrum, J. F. 1954. A study of certain factors of the ecology of the Texas harvester ant, *Pogonomyrmex barbatus* var. *molefaciens* (Buckl.). Ph.D. diss., Agricultural and Mechanical College of Texas.

Marais, E. N. 1937. *The soul of the white ant.* New York: Dodd, Mead, and Company.

Marcus, H. 1953. Estudios mirmecológicos. *Folia Univ. Cochab.* 6:17–68.

Marcus, H., and E. Marcus. 1951. Los nidos y los organos de estridulación y de equilibrio de *Pogonomyrmex marcusi* y de *Dorymyrmex emmaericaellus* (KUSN). *Folia Univ. Cochab.* 5:117–43.

Markl, H., B. Hölldobler, and T. Hölldobler. 1977. Mating behavior and sound production in harvester ants (*Pogonomyrmex*, Formicidae). *Insectes Sociaux* 24 (2):191–212.

Martin, M. M., and T. J. Lieb. 1979. Patterns of fuel utilization by the thoracic muscles of adult worker ants: The use of lipid by a hymenopteran. *Comp. Biochem. Physiol.* 64B:387–90.

Maynard Smith, J., and E. Szathmáry. 1995. *The major transitions in evolution.* New York: W. H. Freeman and Company.

Melander, A. L. 1902. A new silphid beetle from a simple insect-trap. *Psyche* 9 (312):328–29.

Melander, A. L., and C. T. Brues. 1906. The chemical nature of some insect secretions. *Bull. Wisconsin Natural History Society (N.S.)* 4 (1/2):22–36.

Melvin, C. E. 1968. Presence or absence of chemical trail following in the western harvester ant, *Pogonomyrmex occidentalis* (Cresson) (Hymenoptera: Formicidae). Master's thesis, University of Wyoming.

Michener, C. D. 1948. Observations on the mating behavior of harvester ants. *J. New York Entomol. Soc.* 56:239–42.

Mitchell, J. D., and W. D. Pierce. 1912. The ants of Victoria County, Texas. *Proc. Entomol. Soc. Wash.* 14 (1):67–76.

Möglich, M., and B. Hölldobler. 1974. Social carrying behavior and division of labor during nest moving in ants. *Psyche* 81 (2):219–36.

Moggridge, J. T. 1873. *Harvesting ants and trap-door spiders: Notes and observations on their habits and dwellings.* Covent Garden, London, Eng.: L. Reeve and Company.

Moody, J. V., and D. E. Foster. 1979. Notes on the bionomics and nest structure of *Pogonomyrmex maricopa* (Hymenoptera: Formicidae). In *Biological investigations in the Guadalupe Mountains National Park, Texas,* edited by H. H. Genoways and R. J. Baker. National Park Service Proceedings and Transactions Series, no. 4. Washington, D.C.: National Park Service.

Moody, J. V., and O. F. Francke. 1982. Subfamily Myrmicinae. Pt. 1 of *The ants (Hymenoptera: Formicidae) of western Texas.* Texas Tech University Graduate Studies, no. 27. Lubbock: Texas Tech Press.

Morgan, K. Z., and J. E. Turner, eds. 1973. Principles of radiation protection. Huntington, N.Y.: Robert E. Krieger.

Morrill, W. L. 1972. Tool using behavior of *Pogonomyrmex badius* (Hymenoptera: Formicidae). *Florida Entomol.* 55 (1):59–60.

Murphy, P. G., and A. E. Lugo. 1995. Dry forests of Central America and the Caribbean. In *Seasonally dry tropical forests,* edited by S. H. Bullock, H. A. Mooney, and E. Medina. Cambridge: Cambridge University Press.

Nagel, H. G. 1969. Western harvester ants in Kansas: Colony founding, nest structure and function, factors affecting density, and effect on soil formation. Ph.D. diss., Kansas State University.

———. 1971. Water relations of the ant *Pogonomyrmex occidentalis* Cresson. *Proc. Nebr. Acad. Sci. Affil. Soc.* 81:15.

Nagel, H. G., and C. W. Rettenmeyer. 1973. Nuptial flights, reproductive behavior, and colony founding of the western harvester ant, *Pogono-myrmex occidentalis* (Hymenoptera: Formicidae). *J. Kansas Entomol. Soc.* 46 (1):82–101.

do Nascimento, R. R., B. D. Jackson, E. D. Morgan, W. H. Clark, and P. E. Blom. 1993. Chemical secretions of two sympatric harvester ants, *Pogono-myrmex salinus* and *Messor lobognathus*. *J. Chem. Ecology* 19 (9):1993–2005.

Nehrling, H. 1884. Texas und seine Tierwelt. In *Der Zoologische Garten*, edited by F. C. Noll. Frankfurt-am-Main, Germany: Mahlau and Wald-schmidt.

Nelson, C. H. 1988. Note on the phylogenetic systematics of the family Pteronarcyidae (Plecoptera), with a description of the Asian species. *Ann. Entomol. Soc. Am.* 81 (4):560–76.

Nichol, A. A. 1931. Control of the harvester ant. *Univ. Ariz. Coll. Agric. Exp. Sta. Bull.* 138:639–52.

Nielsen, M. G. 1986. Respiratory rates of ants from different climatic areas. *J. Insect Phys.* 32 (2):125–31.

Opler, M. E. 1965. *An Apache life-way: The economic, social, and religious institutions of the Chiricahua Indians.* New York: Cooper Square Publishers.

Oster, G. F., and E. O. Wilson. 1978. *Caste and ecology in the social insects.* Princeton Monographs in Population Biology, no. 12. Princeton, N.J.: Princeton University Press.

Pandazis, G. 1930. Uber die relative ausbildung der Gehirnzentren bei biol-ogisch verschiedenen Ameisenarten. *Z. f. Morphol. u. Ökol. d. Tiere* 18:114–69.

Parish, H. E. 1949. Recent studies on life history and habits of the ear tick. *J. Econ. Entomol.* 42 (3):416–19.

Peeters, C. 1997. Morphologically "primitive" ants: Comparative review of social characters and the importance of queen-worker dimorphism. In *Social behavior in insects and arachnids,* edited by J. C. Choe and B. J. Crespi. Cambridge: Cambridge University Press.

Petralia, R. S., and S. B. Vinson. 1979. Comparative anatomy of the ventral region of ant larvae, and its relation to feeding behavior. *Psyche* 86 (4):375–94.

Pflieger, W. L. 1971. A distributional study of Missouri fishes. *University of Kansas Publications, Museum of Natural History* 20 (3):225–570.

Piek, T., J. O. Schmidt, J. M. DeJong, and P. Mantel. 1989. Kinins in ant venoms: A comparison with venoms of related Hymenoptera. *Comp. Biochem. Physiol.* 92C (1):117–24.

Pinnas, J. L., R. C. Strunk, T. M. Wang, and H. C. Thompson. 1977. Har-vester ant sensitivity: In vitro and in vivo studies using whole body ex-tracts and venom. *J. Allergy Clin. Immunol.* 59 (1):10–16.

Pittaway, A. R. 1991. *Arthropods of medical and veterinary importance: A checklist of preferred names and allied terms.* Wallingford, Oxon, Eng.: CAB International.

Popenoe, E. A. 1904. Pogonomyrmex occidentalis. *Can. Entomol.* 36:360.

Porter, S. D. 1985. *Masoncus* spider: A miniature predator of Collembola in harvester ant colonies. *Psyche* 92 (1):145–50.

Porter, S. D., and C. D. Jorgensen. 1980. Recapture studies of the harvester ant, *Pogonomyrmex owyheei* Cole, using a fluorescent marking technique. *Ecol. Entomol.* 5:263–69.

———. 1981. Foragers of the harvester ant, *Pogonomyrmex owyheei*: A disposable caste? *Behav. Ecol. Sociobiol.* 9:247–56.

Reading of letter sent to the Academy by G. Lincecum, regarding *P. barbatus.* 1866. *Proc. Acad. Nat. Sci. Phil.* 18:101–106.

Remarks on ants. 1877. *Proc. Acad. Nat. Sci. Phil.* 29:304–305.

Rissing, S. W. 1983. Natural history of the workerless inquiline ant *Pogonomyrmex colei* (Hymenoptera: Formicidae). *Psyche* 90:321–32.

———. 1988. Seed-harvester ant association with shrubs: Competition for water in the Mohave Desert? *Ecology* 69 (3):809–13.

Rodgers, G. C., Jr., and N. J. Matyunas, eds. 1994. *Handbook of common poisonings in children.* 3d ed. Elk Grove Village, Ill.: American Academy of Pediatrics.

Rogers, L. E. 1974. Foraging activity of the western harvester ant in the shortgrass plains ecosystem. *Environ. Entomol.* 3:420–24.

———. 1987. Ecology and management of harvester ants in the shortgrass plains. In *Integrated pest management on rangeland: A shortgrass prairie perspective,* edited by J. L. Capinera. Boulder, Colo.: Westview Press.

Roig, F. A., M. M. Gonzalez Loyarte, E. M. Abraham de Vozquez, E. Martinez Carretero, E. Mendez, and V. G. Roig. 1992. Argentina: Desertification hazard mapping of central-western Argentina. In *World atlas of desertification.* New York: Edward Arnold, United Nations Environment Programme.

Ross, H. H. 1973. Evolution and phylogeny. In *History of entomology,* edited by R. F. S. Smith, T. E. Mittler, and C. N. Smith. Palo Alto, Calif.: Annual Reviews.

Rundel, P. W. 1981. The matorral zone of central Chile. In *Mediterranean-type shrublands,* edited by F. Castri, D. W. Goodall, and R. L. Specht. Vol. 11 of *Ecosystems of the world.* New York: Elsevier Scientific Publishing Company.

Santschi, F. 1921. Ponerinae, Dorylinae et quelques autres formicides néotropiques. *Bull. Soc. Vaud. Sc. Nat.* 54 (200):81–103.

Schmidt, J. O. 1986. Chemistry, pharmacology, and chemical ecology of ant venoms. In *Venoms of the Hymenoptera: Biochemical, pharmacologi-*

cal, and behavioural aspects, edited by T. Piek. New York: Academic Press.

————. 1989. Spines and venoms in flora and fauna in the Arizona upland Sonoran Desert and how they act as defenses against vertebrates. In *Special biotic relationships in the arid southwest,* edited by J. O. Schmidt. Albuquerque: University of New Mexico Press.

————. 1990. Chemical and behavioral counterattack. In *Insect defenses,* edited by D. L. Evans and J. O. Schmidt. Albany: State University of New York Press.

Schmidt, J. O., and M. S. Blum. 1978a. A harvester ant venom: Chemistry and pharmacology. *Science* 200:1064–65.

————. 1978b. Pharmacological and toxicological properties of harvester ant, *Pogonomyrmex badius,* venom. *Toxicon* 16:645–51.

————. 1978c. The biochemical constituents of the venom of the harvester ant, *Pogonomyrmex badius. Comp. Biochem. Physiol.* 61C:239–47.

Schmidt, J. O., P. J. Schmidt, and R. R. Snelling. 1986. *Pogonomyrmex occidentalis,* an addition to the ant fauna of Mexico, with notes on other species of harvester ants from Mexico (Hymenoptera: Formicidae). *Southwest. Nat.* 31 (3):395–96.

Schmidt, P. J., and J. O. Schmidt. 1989. Harvester ants and horned lizards predator-prey interactions. In *Special biotic relationships in the arid southwest,* edited by J. O. Schmidt. Albuquerque: University of New Mexico Press.

Schmidt, P. J., W. C. Sherbrooke, and J. O. Schmidt. 1989. The detoxification of ant *(Pogonomyrmex)* venom by a blood factor in horned lizards *(Phrynosoma). Copeia* 3:603–607.

Schmutz, E. M., E. L. Smith, P. R. Ogden, M. L. Cox, J. O. Klemmedson, J. J. Norris, and L. C. Fierro. 1992. Desert grassland. In *Natural grasslands: Introduction and western hemisphere,* edited by R. T. Coupland. Vol. 8A of *Ecosystems of the world.* New York: Elsevier Scientific Publishing Company.

Seger, J. 1996. Exoskeletons out of the closet. *Science* 274:941.

Shapley, H. 1920a. Preliminary report on pterergates in *Pogonomyrmex californicus. Proc. Nat. Acad. Sci.* 6 (12):687–90.

————. 1920b. Note on pterergates in the Californian harvester ant. *Psyche* 27 (4):72–74.

Shattuck, S. O. 1987. An analysis of geographic variation in the *Pogonomyrmex occidentalis* complex (Hymenoptera: Formicidae). *Psyche* 94 (1/2):159–79.

Snelling, R. R. 1981. The taxonomy and distribution of some North American *Pogonomyrmex* and descriptions of two new species (Hymenoptera: Formicidae). *Bull. Southern Calif. Acad. Sci.* 80 (3):97–112.

Snelling, R. R., and C. D. George. 1979. *The taxonomy, distribution, and ecology of California desert ants (Hymenoptera: Formicidae).* U.S. Dept. Interior, Bur. Land Management, Cal. Desert Plant Program.

Spangler, H. G. 1967. Ant stridulations and their synchronization with abdominal movement. *Science* 155 (3770):1687–89.

Spangler, H. G., and C. W. Rettenmeyer. 1966. The function of the ammochaetae or psammophores of harvester ants, *Pogonomyrmex* spp. *J. Kansas Entomol. Soc.* 39 (4):739–45.

Standen, A. 1943. *Insect invaders.* Boston: Houghton Mifflin.

Stoetzel, M. B. 1989. *Common names of insects and related organisms.* Lanham, Md.: Entomological Society of America.

Stories from the spirit world: The legend of the sun. National Public Radio Cassette SA-870112.02/04-C 1987.

Strandtmann, R. W. 1942. On the marriage flight of *Pogonomyrmex comanche* Wheeler (Hymenoptera: Formicidae). *Ann. Entomol. Soc. Amer.* 35 (2): 140.

Strickberger, M. W. 1996. *Evolution.* 2d ed. Sudbury, Mass.: Jones and Bartlett Publishers.

Swainson, W. 1840. *Taxidermy, bibliography, and biography: The cabinet cyclopaedia: Natural history.* London: Longman, Orme, Brown, Green, and Longmans, and John Taylor.

Swofford, D. L. 1993. PAUP: Phylogenetic Analysis Using Parsimony Version 3.1.1. Illinois Natural History Survey, Champaign, Ill.

Taber, S. W. 1994. Labile behavioral evolution in a genus of agricultural pests. *Ann. Entomol. Soc. Am.* 87 (3):311–20.

Taber, S. W., J. C. Cokendolpher, and O. F. Francke. 1988. Karyological study of North American *Pogonomyrmex* (Hymenoptera: Formicidae). *Insectes Sociaux* 35 (1):47–60.

Taber, S. W., and O. F. Francke. 1986. A bilateral gynandromorph of the western harvester ant, *Pogonomyrmex occidentalis* (Hymenoptera: Formicidae). *Southwest. Nat.* 31 (2):274–76.

Taylor, F. 1978. Foraging behavior of ants: Theoretical considerations. *J. Theor. Biol.* 71:541–65.

Turner, C. H. 1909. The mound of *Pogonomyrmex badius* Latrl. and its relation to the breeding habits of the species. *Biol. Bull.* 17 (2):161–69.

Vinson, S. B. 1997. Invasion of the red imported fire ant (Hymenoptera: Formicidae). *Am. Entomol.* (Spring):23–39.

Wallace, A. R. 1879. The agricultural ants of Texas. Review of *The natural history of the agricultural ant of Texas,* by H. C. McCook. *Nature* 20 (517):501.

Warnhoff, E. H., Jr. 1947. *A comparison of the effects of several insecticides on the harvester ant.* Master's thesis, Agricultural and Mechanical College of Texas.

Warren, A., Y. C. Sud, and B. Rozanov. 1996. The future of deserts. *J. Arid Environments* 32:75–89.

Wheeler, G. C., and E. W. Wheeler. 1944. The ants of North Dakota. *No. Dak. Hist. Quar.* 11 (4):231–71.

Wheeler, G. C., and J. Wheeler. 1963. *The ants of North Dakota.* Grand Forks: University of North Dakota Press.

———. 1973. *Ants of Deep Canyon.* Riverside: University of California, Philip L. Boyd Deep Canyon Desert Research Center.

———. 1986. *The ants of Nevada.* Los Angeles: Los Angeles County Museum of Natural History.

Wheeler, W. M. 1900. A study of some Texan Ponerinae. *Biol. Bull.* 2 (1):1–31.

———. 1902a. A new agricultural ant from Texas, with remarks on the known North American species. *Amer. Nat.* 36 (422):85–100.

———. 1902b. New agricultural ants from Texas. *Psyche* 9:387–93.

———. 1902c. A consideration of S. B. Buckley's "North American Formicidae." *Trans. Texas Acad. Sci.* 4 (2):17–31.

———. 1910. *Ants: Their structure, development, and behavior.* Columbia Biological Series, no. 9. New York: Columbia University Press.

———. 1914. New and little known harvesting ants of the genus *Pogonomyrmex. Psyche* 21:149–57.

———. 1928. *The social insects: Their origin and evolution.* New York: Harcourt, Brace, and Company.

Wheeler, W. M., and W. M. Mann. 1914. The ants of Haiti. *Bull. Amer. Mus. Nat. Hist.* 33:1–61.

White, R. E. 1983. A field guide to the beetles of North America. New York: Houghton Mifflin Company.

Whitford, W. G. 1976. Foraging behavior of Chihuahuan Desert harvester ants. *Amer. Midland Nat.* 95 (2):455–58.

Whitford, W. G., and M. Bryant. 1979. Behavior of a predator and its prey: The horned lizard *(Phrynosoma cornutum)* and harvester ants (*Pogonomyrmex* spp.). *Ecology* 60 (4):686–94.

Whitford, W. G., and G. Ettershank. 1975. Factors affecting foraging activity in Chihuahuan Desert harvester ants. *Environ. Entomol.* 4 (5):689–96.

Whitford, W. G., G. S. Forbes, and G. I. Kerley. 1995. Diversity, spatial variability, and functional roles of invertebrates in desert grassland ecosystems. In *The desert grassland,* edited by M. P. McClaran and T. R. Van Devender. Tucson: University of Arizona Press.

Whitford, W. G., P. L. Johnson, and J. Ramirez. 1976. Comparative ecology of the harvester ants *Pogonomyrmex barbatus* (F. Smith) and *Pogonomyrmex rugosus* (Emery). *Insectes Sociaux* 23 (2):117–32.

Whiting, M. J., J. R. Dixon, and R. C. Murray. 1993. Spatial distribution of a population of Texas horned lizards (*Phrynosoma cornutum:* Phrynosomatidae) relative to habitat and prey. *Southwest. Nat.* 38 (2):150–54.

Wight, J. R., and J. T. Nichols. 1966. Effects of harvester ants on production of a saltbush community. *J. Range Management* 19 (2):68–71.

Wildermuth, V. L., and E. G. Davis. 1931. The red harvester ant and how to subdue it. *USDA Farmer's Bull.* 1668.

Willard, J. R. 1964. Biological activities of the harvester ant, *Pogonomyrmex owyheei* Cole, in central Oregon. Master's thesis, Oregon State University.

Wilson, E. O. 1963. The social biology of ants. *Ann. Rev. Entomol.* 8:345–68.

———. 1971. *The insect societies.* Cambridge: Harvard University Press, Belknap Press.

Wilson, E. O., and W. H. Bossert. 1963. Chemical communication among animals. *Recent Progress in Hormone Research* 19:673–716.

Wilson, E. O., N. I. Durlach, and L. M. Roth. 1958. Chemical releasers of necrophoric behavior in ants. *Psyche* 65 (4):108–14.

Winton, W. M. 1915. A preliminary note on the food habits and distribution of the Texas horned lizards. *Science* 41 (1065):797–98.

Worthing, C. R., and R. J. Hance, eds. 1991. *The pesticide manual.* 9th ed. Farnham, Surrey, England: British Crop Protection Council.

Wu, H. J. 1990. Disk clearing behavior of the red harvester ant, *Pogonomyrmex barbatus* Smith. *Bull. Inst. Zool. Acad. Sinica* 29 (3):153–64.

Wyman, L. C. 1965. *The Red Antway of the Navaho.* Santa Fe, N.M.: Museum of Navajo Ceremonial Art.

Wyman, L. C., and F. L. Bailey. 1964. *Navaho Indian ethnoentomology.* University of New Mexico Publications in Anthropology, no. 12. Albuquerque: University of New Mexico Press.

Young, J. H., and D. E. Howell. 1954. The mating swarm of the Texas harvester ant (*Pogonomyrmex barbatus,* F. Smith). *Proc. Okla. Acad. Sci.* 35:60–62.

———. 1964. Ants of Oklahoma. Stillwater: Oklahoma State University Experiment Station.

Zelade, R. 1986. Feasting on asphalt. *Texas Monthly* (Aug.):92–94.

Index

Scientific names and pages containing relevant figures appear in italics.

buffalo wallows, 22

calcium cyanide, 128
California harvester ant *(Pogonomy-rmex californicus)*: abnormalities, 74; compared to *Pogonomyrmex snellingi,* 172, 173; competing harvesters, 50; in data matrix, 165; emigration, 26; etymology of name, 133; in evolutionary tree, 76; foraging behavior, 40, 41, 43; habitus and distribution, 107; heat tolerance, 14–15; and hot deserts, 78; identification, 140, 151; larva, 29; metabolism, 69; nest closure, 23–24; nest entrance movement, 56; nesting sites, 18; nest structure, 22–23; pest status, 125, 127; radiation resistance, 70–71; and rough harvester ant, 10; and spiders, 47; tending brood, 29; and termites, 35
California poppy bush, 42–43
cannibalism, 35
carbon bisulphide, 128
carpenter ants, 83
carrying behavior, 42
character data, 155–68
character-optimization procedures, 86, 156
chemistry, 58–62
chirality, 59
chitin, 55–56
chitinase, 69
chlordane, 128
chromosomes, 31, 70–72, 81, 90, 92
circadian rhythms, 69
circumocular whorls. *See* eye loops
clade, 89
cladistics, 77
classification, 89–92

clearing (surrounding nest area), 20, 21–22
Clypeadon wasp, 49–50
clypeal lobes, 87
clypeal plate, 143–44
cockroach, 51
Cole, A. C., XVII, 90, 169
Cole's harvester ant. *See Pogono-myrmex colei*
colony raiding, 47
Comanche harvester ant *(Pogonomy-rmex comanche)*: abnormalities, 74; compared to *Pogonomyrmex snellingi,* 173; in data matrix, 166; diet, 36–37; etymology of name, 133; in evolutionary tree, 76; and fire ants, 127; habitat, 15; habitus and distribution, 109; identification, 139–40, mating swarm, 63; nest, 37; nest closure, 23, 24, 25; foraging behavior, 41; and spiders, 47–48; type locality, 10; worker, 4, 5, 6, 11
Combat, 128
common names, 5, 131–34
communication, 58–62
competition, 50
computer analysis, 77, 155–56
conservative characters, 88
convoluted gland, 58, 60
Cope's Rule, 88–89
couplets, 142
Cretaceous period, 84
Croizat, L., 84

Darling, K., 9
Darwin, C., XV–XVI, 30, 32–35, 87
DDT, 128
deaths (from harvester stings), 53
desert harvester ant *(Pogonomyrmex desertorum)*: and competing harvesters, 50; in data matrix,

hexachlorocyclohexane, 128
Hispaniola. *See* Haiti
histamine, 60
Hölldobler, B., 129, 142
homing signal, 60–61
homoplasy, 92
homosexual encounters, 64
horned lizard, 4, 9, 44–45, 67
horned toad. *See* horned lizard
horseshoe crab beetle, 51–52
hot deserts (origins of), 78
houseguests, 51–53
house pests, 127
Huachuca harvester. *See Pogonomyrmex huachucanus*
humans and harvester ants, 44, 50,
53–55, 125–29
humidity preference, 68
hyaluronidase, 60
hybridization, 65
hydramethylnon, 128
hydrocarbons, 61
Hylomyrma, 77, 90, 142, 144, 172,
173
Hylomyrma reitteri, 12, 76, 77, 78,
124, 164

identifying harvester ants, 135–54
inbreeding, 63
individual foraging, 39–40
inquilines. *See* social parasites
insecticides, 25, 26, 127, 128
intelligence, 69–70
intermorphs, 65–66

J&J Multipurpose Insect Bait, 128
jaws, 55. *See also* anatomy
jimson weed, 43

kangaroo rats, 55
karyotype, 71,72. *See also* chromosomes
Kepone, 128

keys (identification), 141–54. *See also*
identifying harvester ants
kinins, 60

labile characters, 88
larva, 29, 38, 39, 52, 61, 64, 66, 104
larval blood (as food of ants), 37
Latreille, P., 37–38
LD50, 54
leaf-cutter ants, 9, 10
learning, 69
Leidy, J., 34
lek, 62–64
life expectancy, 67–68
Lincecum, G., 17, 33–35, 34, 59, 61,
63–64, 71, 87
Lincecum, J., 34
"Lincecum Hypothesis," 17, 33–35.
See also Lincecum, G.
lipase, 60
lipids, 60, 69
London purple, 128
low temperature adaptations, 68–69
lugs, 142

McCook, H. C., 34, 35, 59, 61, 66
MacKay, W. P., 15, 37, 66
majority rule consensus tree, 76, 91
major worker, 67, 72, 103, 108, 145.
See also Florida harvester; *Pogonomyrmex coarctatus;* polymorphism
males, 28, 29, 30–31, 66, 70, 161–
62. *See also* family relatedness
mandibular gland, 58, 59, 62
Manica, 142
mapping characters, 77, 156
Marcus's harvester ant. *See Pogonomyrmex marcusi*
Maricopa harvester ant *(Pogonomyrmex maricopa):* abnormalities,
74; and competing harvesters,
50; in data matrix, 166; emigra-

pheromone. *See* alarm pheromone; homing signal; recruitment pheromone

Philadelphia Academy of Sciences, 34

phosphatase, 60

phospholipase, 60

Phrynosoma. See horned lizard

phylogeny. *See* evolutionary tree

piperonyl butoxide, 128

plains blind snake, 46

planidium, 50

plant lice. *See* aphids

Pliocene land bridge, 83

Pogonomyrmex: character evolution, 88; etymology of name, 132; in evolutionary tree, 76, 83; food processing, 39; generic status 90–92; as harvester ants, XV, 4, 5–6; identification, 135, 141–45; intelligence, 69–70; origin of, 84, 86; pest status of, 125

Pogonomyrmex anergismus: characteristics of, 48, 65; in data matrix, 168; etymology of name, 132; in evolutionary tree, 91; habitus and distribution, 101; hosts of, 30; identification, 140, 145; sexuals and host, 89

Pogonomyrmex anzensis, 18, 19, 76, 78, 87, 101, 132, 140, 165

Pogonomyrmex apache: abnormalities, 74; in data matrix, 165, 168; etymology of name, 132; in evolutionary tree, 76, 91; foraging behavior, 41; habitus and distribution, 102; and hot deserts, 78; houseguests, 53; identification, 139, 149; and packrat garbage piles, 79; and *Pogonomyrmex snellingi,* 173; and termites, 35–36

Pogonomyrmex atratus, 76, 102, 132, 138, 152, 165

Pogonomyrmex badius. See Florida harvester ant

Pogonomyrmex barbatus. See red harvester ant

Pogonomyrmex bicolor, 76, 91, 104, 133, 139, 148, 165, 168

Pogonomyrmex bigbendensis, 76, 87, 105, 133, 139, 148, 165

Pogonomyrmex bispinosus, 76, 91, 105, 133, 151, 165

Pogonomyrmex brevispinosus, 76, 106, 133, 140, 150, 165

Pogonomyrmex bruchi, 72, 76, 106, 133, 153, 165

Pogonomyrmex californicus. See California harvester ant

Pogonomyrmex carbonarius, 76, 107, 133, 151, 152, 166

Pogonomyrmex catanlilensis, 76, 108, 133, 153, 166

Pogonomyrmex coarctatus: brain, 69; colony population, 29; competition, 50; in data matrix, 166; diet, 37; ecological release, 87; etymology of name, 133; in evolutionary tree, 76; food processing, 39; foraging behavior, 32; habitus and distribution, 108; identification, 145, 153; origin of, 82, 87; polymorphism, 72; and pseudoscorpions, 48; size, 29–30, 37; sting, 54; "sunning" behavior, 48

Pogonomyrmex colei, 30, 48, 65, 90, 91, 109, 133, 140, 145, 168. *See also Pogonomyrmex anergismus;* social parasites

Pogonomyrmex comanche. See Comanche harvester ant

Pogonomyrmex desertorum. See desert harvester ant

root. *See* evolutionary tree

rough harvester ant *(Pogonomyrmex rugosus)*: cannibalism, 35; chemistry, 61; coloration, 66; competing harvesters, 25, 50; desiccation resistance, 68; in data matrix, 167, 168; drinking, 38; emigration, 26; etymology of name, 134; in evolutionary tree, 76, 91; exoskeleton, 68; foraging behavior, 40, 41; habitus and distribution, *118*; houseguests, 51–52; hybridization, 65; identification, 139, 148; and infected seeds, 39; intelligence, 69–70; learning, 69; in mixed nests, 30; mounds, 19; nest, *10*; nest closure, 24; nest population, 30; nesting sites, 18; parasites of, 48, 89–90; parasitoid of, 49; and the plains blind snake, 46; queen, 66, 68; raids, 47; size, 66; stridulation, 62; and termites, 35; trails, 21; weight, 41; worker, 89

sage grouse, 64

Santschi, F. 87

scientific names, 5, 131–34

scuttle fly (Phoridae), 50–51

seeds: and the nest clearing, 21; as dietary preference, 13, 32–33, 86; dispersal, 42–43; germination, 39; and the "Lincecum Hypothesis," 33–35; pests of, 125–26; poisoned, 127; preparation, 38–39; and rodents, 55; storage, 15, 20, 32–33, 37–38, 67. *See also* diet

segments (evolution of), 88

sentinels, 57

sesquiterpenoid, 61

setae, 88

sexual production, 64

sexuals (keys to), 142

Shapley, H., 74

shared, derived characters, 77, 142

Shattuck, S., 142

silverfish, 51–52. *See also* houseguests

sister species, 81

Skrjabinoptera phrynosoma, 48

sleep, 63, 67

Snelling, R. R., 169, 173

Snelling's harvester ant. *See Pogonomyrmex snellingi*

social parasites, 30, 48, 65, 85, 89–91, 145, 168, 140. *See also Pogonomyrmex anergismus; Pogonomyrmex colei*

sodium cyanide, 128

species B. *See Pogonomyrmex species B*

species drawings, 93–124

spermatheca, 64–65

spiders, 24, 47–48, 51, 61

spines, 55–56, 74

spiracle valve, 68

springtails, 51

Standen, A., 128

sternal gland, 58

stinger (sting), 6–8, 53–55, 88

stridulation, 61–62, 64

"sunning," 48–49

synapomorphy. *See* shared, derived characters

tasting harvester ants, 59

teeth (evolution of), 87

termites, 35–36, 51, 53, 127

thief ants, 51

three-awn, 33

tool use, 42, 46, 56

toxaphene, 128

trail pheromone. *See* recruitment pheromone

trails, 21, 40

trash concealment, 56
"trembling," 128
trophic eggs, 35
trunk trails, 21

Velsicol 1068, 128
venom, 54, 55, 60. *See also* sting
vicariance, 75

Wallace, A. R., 34
water content, 66–67
weight, 66
western harvester ant *(Pogono-myrmex occidentalis)*: abnormalities, 74; and aphids, 42; benefits of, 127; compared to *Pogonomyrmex snellingi,* 173; in data matrix, 166, 168; desiccation resistance, 68; drinking, 38; eggs as food, 35; emigration, 25; enemies of, 46–47; etymology of name, 134; in evolutionary tree, 76, 91; in fiction, 9; food processing, 39; foraging behavior, 32, 40–41, 42; gynandromorph, 73; habitat preference, 13–14, 17; habitus and distribution, 116; houseguests, 51; humidity preference, 68; hybridization, 65; identification, 140, 149; and infected seeds, 39; life expectancy, 68; mating swarms, 63; mound/nest construction, 5, 17, 19–23, 88; nest closure, 23–24; nest population, 28, 30; nest repair, 21; origin of, 80, 88; parasitoid of, 49; pest status, 125–26; queen, 68; range expansion, 17; recruitment pheromone, 60; seed storage, 32–33
Wheeler, W. M., 10–11, 15, 16, 27, 56, 63, 64
Wheeler's harvester ant. *See Pogono-myrmex wheeleri*
Whitehead, A. N., 10–11
Williston's Rule, 88
Wilson, E. O., 59, 129, 142
wing removal, 64
workers, 30–32, 48, 62, 65, 66–68, 74, 156–60. *See also* family relatedness

Zuni Indians, 8